STOP HITTING SNOOZE

BRANT SHRIMPLIN

LEGACY
launch pad
PUBLISHING

CONTENTS

Foreword	viii
Prologue	1
Introduction	3
Chapter 1—Defining Your Purpose	7
Chapter 2—What is Happiness and How Do We Achieve It?	25
Chapter 3—Leaving Your Old Identity Behind	49
Chapter 4—The Force of Friends	65
Chapter 5—You Always Control the Outcome	91
Chapter 6—Give to Give	103
Chapter 7—Be Endlessly Grateful	115
Conclusion	125
Acknowledgments	129
About the Author	132
About the Publisher	134

Copyright © 2024 by Brant Shrimplin.

All rights reserved.

No part of this book may be reproduced in any form or by any electronic or mechanical means, including information storage and retrieval systems, without written permission from the author, except for the use of brief quotations in a book review.

Cover Design by: onegraphica.com

ISBN: 978-1-964377-24-7 (ebook)

ISBN: 978-1-964377-23-0 (paperback)

ISBN: 978-1-964377-28-5 (hardcover)

1,000 sets of braces for 1,000 kids in 1,000 days. There are moments in time that are life-changing. For many kids, this comes in the form of braces, a confidence-inspiring moment during life's pivotal years. Unfortunately, the ability to receive this gift is out of reach for many. Please join us in our mission to change that one smile at a time.

I dedicate this book to my amazing wife, Lindsay, and my two children, Avery and Beckett. Thank you for inspiring me to be my best in everything that I do.

FOREWORD

This foreword was hatched while masterminding in the most magical place on Earth created by one of the planet's greatest magic men—Sir Richard Branson.

Branson's Necker Island, his home and wonderland for visionaries who visit, is where I was so incredibly grateful to meet Brant Shrimplin.

My wife, Dr. Sarah Breen, and I came to Necker as part of the very first ReblDads event, where dad-entrepreneurs met to discuss dad life, entrepreneur life and the ups and downs of both. A mix of mastermind and the greatest experiences imaginable.

I have high intuition and could tell Brant was a unicorn, even among unicorns. He had a magical blend of genius heart and genius brain. He puts friends and family first, then blends business, finance and more to create life plans. Purpose plans.

He learned this from birth, from the extreme love and guidance of both his parents, and he would learn more

FOREWORD

from partnering with his father later in life with his first company. That is true greatness.

After we left Necker, Brant sent me a series of four pictures that showed the absolute genius of his brain and heart and soul. On those pictures were a life plan—a purpose plan, really—for a friend of his. Brant had written a Biblical-like mantra that showcased his talent. I recommended he highlight this rare talent with this book. So, here we are.

As background, I spend my entire life either with Sarah and our two sons, Jake and Chase, or connecting with the world's top visionaries to understand them and, more importantly, learn their best practices to use in my life and companies. Very, very, very rarely does something resonate with me the way Brant's words and messaging did. It hit me like a lightning bolt.

In short, Brant is a master of mind, soul, heart and finance. This book will help you on your way to that mastery as well.

—Justin Breen, Jan. 27, 2024

It was a race against time. As I sped past cars, I couldn't help but think about the things I might hear that day. I wanted all the answers but knew that I probably wouldn't get them. How long would it take, how would things change and what lessons would be learned? None of it matters now, I thought as I swerved across the lanes and occasionally looked down at my GPS. *I just have to get there.*

My wife and I had always had this phrase, one we'd muttered to each other since shortly after college: *Simple is too easy.* On that day, simplicity was all I wanted, since I knew that what was about to come would be anything but.

I finally arrived, grabbed my notepad and rushed into the hospital, not exactly sure which direction I needed to go. As I raced down the hall and turned the corner, I saw Scott, a former hockey pro and one of my best friends, and I knew I had made it in time. He smiled and I smiled back, trying to look as strong and reassuring as I could.

"It's about time," he said. "We're going to get started. Follow me."

Little did I know the things I learned that day would change my life forever.

INTRODUCTION

I have never been short on empathy. In fact, sometimes I wonder why I care so much. It doesn't matter if it's the stranger wandering the street alone, the kid without money in Mexico or a close friend in a time of crisis; I've always felt compelled to jump in and help. I tend to follow my heart and create a game plan later, which, ironically, has always led to the best results.

It was never a lifelong dream of mine to become an author. In fact, I hadn't even read a book in several years before starting to write this one. But as my friend Justin Breen calmly told me, "You have to do this to help others." That became a calling of sorts, and my next several weeks were spent writing down the most important messages I wanted to relay to an audience they could impact most. The audience I had in mind was anyone seeking to become the very best version of themselves: those who hoped to learn, share and to have a positive influence on the world around them.

For the majority of my life thus far, I've spent my time providing advice and guidance to fellow entrepreneurs, executives of NYSE-listed companies, founders of successful startups, consultants to Forbes 100 members, large scale real estate developers, specialized physicians, custom home builders, aerospace engineers and several others in between. I've realized that while success is a common thread among those I've worked with, often that success didn't translate into having a sense of purpose, balance or clearly defined values. Oftentimes, those qualities prove to be elusive.

In thinking about the people I have impacted and those who have impacted me, it became clear I needed to share the details that had made those experiences stay with me. I thought about the lives that had transformed and the reasons behind those transformations. The end result of those reflections are detailed in the pages ahead—in stories about overcoming challenges, having relentless optimism, defining one's purpose and, ultimately, transforming into the best version of ourselves we possibly can.

Being able to do all that means responding to life's circumstances with understanding and viewing every scenario as an opportunity for growth. It's about becoming transparent to negative emotions so they can pass right through you. After all, emotions like resentment are a waste of time, and we have no time to waste. It's about realizing that if we stop hitting snooze and take some time to evaluate where we are and where we're headed, life can be much more fulfilling and free.

In life, you realize over time that everything has meaning, good and bad. The challenge is to get to a point that no matter what happens in your life, you are able to respond in a positive way immediately. You radiate light and become an endless source of hope and understanding for those who cross your path. There is a road map to get there, one that includes all the key beliefs I hold close.

Those beliefs have guided me in my life and have helped others gain clarity in otherwise blurred circumstances. After helping many others gain perspective by coming back to these beliefs, I was encouraged to share them with the world to extend my reach. After all, if we don't leave the world in a better place than where we entered it, how can we truly say we lived?

—Brant Shrimplin, 2024

CHAPTER 1—DEFINING YOUR PURPOSE

Purpose is everything, and everything starts with your purpose.

Why are you here? What is your calling? What lessons do you want to teach? What can be learned? Why are you doing what you are doing? Who do you want to be? What do you want to do?

Defining your purpose is a key starting point in determining who you are, where you are and where you want to go. Many of us struggle with this concept: Why am I here and what am I supposed to be doing? Though it may be hard to define, without purpose, we become directionless—and very few people enjoy being lost.

Your purpose is not the same thing as your goals. Goals are specific achievements that *align* with your purpose but are not your purpose in and of themselves.

Your purpose is not the same thing as your values. Your values are the things you view as most important in your life. They are critical for defining your purpose, but they are still distinct from it. To illustrate, some value "success" or "hard work", but personal achievement and career are not the same as true purpose. Work is simply a medium or a vehicle toward fulfilling a purpose.

Since so many people struggle to define the concept of purpose, few ever take the time to do it. They know there are key things that are important to them—such as being a good parent, a good friend or a good person—but rolling these into one ultimate reason to exist generally doesn't happen.

Purpose is certainly not an easy thing to define, and it is a challenge you must work your way up to facing. To answer any profound question, we must start by answering smaller ones first.

To tackle purpose, I had to start by thinking about the moments in my life that made me feel the best about myself. In other words, the moments that gave me *sustained fulfillment*, not just temporary joy. When I say sustained fulfillment, I'm talking about the kind of feeling that does not erode the more we do it. It is easy to clarify things that give us the same level of satisfaction every time versus things that have diminishing returns.

For example, purchasing things (when one is able) can bring great temporary satisfaction. If you have ever worked hard for something and then were finally able to afford it, making that purchase for the first time is something you will probably never forget. For me, it was my first set of golf clubs when I was 12 years old. I worked all summer to save up $275, and in the fall, I walked into MC Sports and bought them.

I can still picture the way they shined on the wall at

the store. I remember gently taking them down and proudly walking up to the register to purchase them, which brought me so much joy. It was the very first significant thing I bought for myself, and I will never forget it—but you can only buy your first set of golf clubs for the first time once.

Over time, those one-time purchases do not bring the same joy as they do the first time, which is natural. As you continue to accumulate things and buy more stuff, gradually, you get diminishing returns. "Things" become less and less rewarding each time. After all, working hard and being able to purchase your first car or your first home typically holds much more importance than buying your second home or your fifth car.

While trying to answer this question of sustained fulfillment, some people might believe that travel could be an answer. This may seem plausible on its surface, but as those who have been fortunate enough to travel to many places know, what truly makes you feel fulfilled is not necessarily travel itself but the people you meet, the shared connections with family or friends or the ability to tell others about what you've seen. Like work, travel is just a vehicle to help fulfill some purpose.

The bottom line is this: To truly achieve sustained fulfillment, I believe what you do has to benefit others and not just yourself, as simply providing joy for one person can only take you so far.

The moments in my life that brought me the most joy were when I was helping someone else feel better about themselves or giving to someone else. That giving did not necessarily mean giving money, but rather doing something to elevate somebody else's day: giving them a compliment, an unexpected gift or calling them to let them know I cared. Simple things, no doubt, but things that made me feel good because I knew they were making others feel good. That truly provided a sustained, positive feeling.

I started and have continued my career in the financial services industry, specifically trading stocks in the public markets. It is often assumed that a career in financial services is all about numbers, rates of return, graphs and charts (in other words: dry and boring). But a financial advisor is much more of a life coach and counselor; after all, finances often affect one's well-being (though ironically, having a sense of well-being has very little to do with having amazing finances).

I have been fortunate to have countless conversations over the years with those in a wide range of professions, including successful entrepreneurs, teachers, physicians, trade workers, C-suite executives and everyone in between. My clients and colleagues have given me great perspective on sustained fulfillment and the difference between what truly brought them joy and what they *thought* would bring them joy.

I had a recent discussion with a successful ophthalmologist who felt that owning and running her own eye care practice would bring her sustained fulfillment. After chasing this "dream" for several years, she realized that deep down, simply helping her patients with something as important as their vision was what *really* gave her sustained fulfillment. It wasn't the specifics of hiring or mentoring doctors, running the books or managing a practice. It was being a great doctor for the purpose of helping others, which is why she headed down the path in the first place.

Ultimately, answering the purpose question is quite simple: What do you love most about each and every day, or what have you done in your past that made you feel sustained fulfillment (as differentiated from the temporary joys and quick fixes)?

When you create the space to think about these things, you may realize you are living the life you *thought* you wanted to live, but it isn't a life of sustained fulfillment. It is not defined by purpose, something that will carry you through all phases of life. You see, when you clearly define your purpose, you can quickly identify the actions that are aligned with it and eliminate those that are not.

I always knew why I was here: to help others in any way that I could. I was asked about my purpose while attending a conference at the University of Chicago, and the answer immediately popped into my head as I followed these thoughts:

> *The more I learn, the more that I can teach*
> *(helping others).*
> *The more I earn, the more I can give away*
> *(impact).*
> *We **must** leave the world in a better place*
> *than when we entered it.*

I live each day with these thoughts front-of-mind. Whenever I am considering tackling a new project, such as writing this book, I ask myself, "Does this align with my purpose?" If not, why should it even be considered?

Projects take time, and time is our most precious commodity, the one thing we cannot get back. If we are to consider spending our time on something or someone, it must align with our purpose to be time well-spent.

Another important question related to purpose is, "Who do I want to be?" That one is easy for me: I want to be someone who learns new things, tries them out and brings them back to other people to share (if they were successful). I have done this in many areas of my life, including but not limited to my work.

Once you can define your purpose, it will help to answer another difficult question, which is: "What makes me different?" When I was first presented with this question, I had a very hard time answering it. I immediately blurted out, "I'm caring, I'm empathetic, I'm driven, I'm [insert common trait of many people]." However, once I took the time to think about my values, my purpose and the moments that brought me sustained fulfillment, what made me unique became clear to me:

I can lead people to places they didn't know they needed to go.

Once you identify the things that bring you sustained fulfillment, you can think about why those things give you that feeling. Doing so means starting to shape your values, the things we view as most important in our lives.

Some common feedback I have received related to values is that some values are simply *desires*—such as wanting to be a great parent, be great to our parents, be successful, be a good friend, work on one's faith, strive for personal development or stay in shape.

Often, the desire is simply wanting to be *seen* as a good person, which can limit you from your truest values and purpose. It's critical to define your values to understand who you are. Only after you can define who you are will you be able to understand how to take your superpowers and share them with the world.

Your values can help you be great, but your *purpose* allows you to make everyone around you better. Once you clearly define why you are here, you will no longer be competing with others. Instead, you'll be sharing the valuable things you've learned with those who are trying to get where you are.

When you think about your values, you can easily check off at least a few things you view as most important. However, you cannot just think about *what* is important. You must dig deeper into *why* these things are important.

For example, I inherently knew my friends were important, but the why didn't dawn on me until I went through periods in my life where I noticed how critical it was to have a group of friends to lean on. Similarly, many of us inherently know that family is important, but until we get older and see how some family members shape our lives and successes, it's difficult to truly appreciate.

My family, friends, physical and mental well-being, faith and career all tie into my purpose: The more I learn, the more I can teach; the more I earn, the more I can give away to help make the world a better place—and we *must* leave the world in a better place than where we entered it.

If you develop good relationships with your family and

friends, you are constantly learning from and supporting each other. Your friends and family are often the first people that you learn from, bounce ideas off and share lessons with. These people are our first test groups, if you will, in trying to understand if our thoughts and feelings are ready for prime time.

If you have good relationships with your friends and family, it naturally helps with your mental well-being. After all, how can we be happy and productive if the most important people around us are struggling? If we are not physically fit and feeling well, how can we expect to function at our highest ability when learning or teaching? If we are fixated on our own negative feelings, we aren't focused on what we can do for others.

Finally, for those of us who find value in giving back (especially at scale), it's important to think about how we can maximize our careers to be able to touch as many people as possible. To make a certain level of impact, giving back takes resources—and having those resources makes giving back significantly more attainable.

For example, if I had only focused on trading stocks over my career, I would not have continuously learned about other ways to invest. That, in turn, would have prevented me from teaching others about new ways to invest, which would have prevented me from having the same economic impact on peoples' lives that I'm able to have today. But to push myself into those new areas, it took family support. For me, that family influence came in the form of my first cousin and partner, Tom.

Tom is my cousin, but he is more like a brother to me. He had a vision of adding venture capital and commercial real estate to our traditional stock and bond offerings. He had learned about these things while getting his MBA from the University of Chicago and wanted to teach me what he had learned.

With Tom (left)

Being the savant that he is, he wanted to build his own platform, which we started doing shortly after we partnered. As it always is with new things, I was unsure and a little afraid of what would ultimately come of our venture, but I enjoyed learning and hoped it would be something we could use to help others.

With the help of a University of Chicago classmate of Tom's, we launched our first venture capital fund in 2018, the Community Access Fund. Had Tom not had the vision to invest in venture capital, and had that concept not aligned with my purpose of learning and teaching others, I would not be where I am today. Oftentimes, learning before being able to teach takes risk, which was certainly the case for me and Tom. Still, we believed it was important to invest our own capital first before rolling the concept out to others.

Because of my strong belief in my purpose, when Tom approached me about this concept and I was faced with doing something I had never done, I was able to overcome that fear and trust that it was going to have meaning, good or bad. Without having the courage to take the risk of investing my own capital first, we would not have been able to teach others about all the wonderful things we ultimately discovered.

Today, Tom and I, along with our long-term partners, now have multiple venture funds and invest with over 40 founders working on critical projects that we believe have the potential to change the world. Again, this aligns with the third part of my purpose: "To leave the world in a better place than we found it." So, by intertwining my work with my purpose and not simply working to work, I've been able to grow and expand my reach.

Like so many entrepreneurs tend to do, after adding in venture capital, we naturally asked ourselves, "What's next?" For us it was commercial real estate, since it carried so many benefits for investors due to factors such as favorable tax laws. Just like we had with venture capital, we wanted to solve the problem ourselves—but not before we tested it.

We started by buying an office building that would become the home of our public markets company, 626 Financial. At the time, it felt like a giant leap for us. We had not invested much in commercial real estate before and had to bootstrap our very first office building for $1.5 million dollars.

The building had 22 offices, and we only needed five, so we had our work cut out for us. We needed to fill the building with other tenants to be successful. We quickly did that, and the process of doing it taught us how the tenant side of the commercial real estate market worked firsthand. After seeing what we had accomplished, we had the confidence to do it again—and bought another office building next door that had a long-term, national tenant in it.

We learned a lot by purchasing these buildings: how to draft leases, interact with tenants, use QuickBooks effectively to track expenses, negotiate, use favorable tax laws to increase our margins and many other lessons.

Once our buildings grew in value, it created an opportunity to expand and invest in larger projects. Tom started to build out a multi-family portfolio in Detroit with a childhood friend of his and now has over 250 units and lots of exciting things going on there. I started to expand my portfolio to include assisted living and memory care, something that was introduced to me by a real estate mentor and friend, Tim. In fact, it was Tim who gave me the opportunity to buy my very first assisted living facility from his family.

While we had great success buying and expanding our real estate portfolio, only when we started to teach others about the benefits of owning real estate did it become truly rewarding. We started by helping individual families with real estate solutions, but we realized that if we wanted to have a greater impact, we needed to think bigger and expand.

As I thought about this, I remembered that Tim owned many buildings scattered throughout Michigan. Perhaps he would be open to selling us *all* of his buildings. It was like a light bulb went off in my head. I'll never forget the moment I called him—it was on a Friday in September 2022 as I was driving to a local coffee shop.

"Tim, what would you think about putting a deal together where we partner our investors with your family's portfolio of facilities?" I asked, barely able to get the words out fast enough. "I believe we can work out an economic model that benefits everyone—the investors, your family and our team for structuring and managing the deal."

Tim thought for only seconds before responding.

"Brant, I think that could work out great," he said. "And actually, many seller/operators like us have been approached from national companies wanting to do this exact thing, but I never considered it because I didn't want to sell and work with a national firm. I want to work with someone local, whose thoughts and ideas are aligned with mine." Within days of our call, we had a basic structure for our next business, and we jumped right in.

We successfully built and launched our first real estate fund just a few months later, and we continue to buy assisted living facilities to this day. We also have a plan to scale this in a meaningful way to benefit both our investors and society at large by tying our philanthropic beliefs into our future funds. It is all part of our continued effort to *leave this world a better place than we found it.*

My point is this: Had we not taken the risk ourselves first, and had these projects not aligned with our purpose, we would have never learned something new or been able to teach and help others. The risks we took evolved into a win-win for many other people, but we couldn't have taken those risks if we hadn't had a clear sense of purpose. Without those pieces in place, we would not be where we are today.

We are very grateful for the success we have had, and it took a lot of people working collectively to help us to get there. Widespread success cannot be accomplished without first believing in yourself, and in turn, having many others believe in your success as well. Once you can do this, it becomes obvious that there are great responsibilities to success. A lot of it depends on giving, which is a big part of our focus now.

After continually thinking about what impact we could make by giving to others, we decided to start a foundation and began making regular contributions to it. We started to think about how we wanted to direct our help—

which is not easy, as there are so many great causes to give to. Our first idea was simple and was spurred on by my daughter, who was a middle school student at the time.

Middle school is a time of great change and development, which for many kids includes getting braces. Braces provide a big confidence boost, which I experienced firsthand. As a child, I had the most crooked teeth anyone had ever seen, and had I not been able to get braces, it could have had a lifelong impact on my self-confidence and self-image (I was fortunate my family was able to afford them, as they are often quite costly).

Bring on the braces! (left); The early years (right)

As I met some of my daughter's middle school friends, I noticed that some of them were beaming with pride with their teeth straightened after braces—and some were not, since their families couldn't afford them. After thinking back on my own experiences, I decided I had found the first idea for the philanthropic foundation: providing braces for kids whose families couldn't afford them.

After doing some research, we found that orthodontics was not as easy as slapping on a pair of braces. Oftentimes, kids who needed braces also needed dental work before the braces could be applied. Having said that, it was still possible—and we are actively working on how to evolve our process to help as many kids as we can.

Our second idea for philanthropy came after Justin Breen introduced me to Randy, a fellow entrepreneur who had started many companies, one of which was in real estate. For his part, Justin is a unique and talented individual, one who doesn't focus on small talk but on spotting talents in people and then making meaningful connections to change the world. And in Randy, he had made another perfect connection.

Like me, Randy constantly looks for ways to give back. After talking to him, he told me how he always donated $10 for each door of each apartment he developed to serve the greater good. He figured that doing that and teaching other real estate developers about it would create a massive impact for causes that were important to him. Similarly, Randy encouraged us to think about how we could better intertwine business with giving, which immediately got us thinking about our assisted living real estate fund.

We started to think about how we could expand our reach beyond kids with braces. Soon, we were thinking about the needs of seniors, the same seniors who were driving the value of our assisted living investments. While assisted living is amazing for those who need it (of whom there will be millions as the Baby Boomers age), it is primarily private pay and thus often unaffordable, with an average price point of nearly $5,000 a month. As Tom and I were talking with Randy, an idea popped into Tom's head: We could direct part of our foundation's profits to help seniors afford assisted living services who otherwise wouldn't be able to.

With a refined vision for our philanthropic arm, our fund became not only an opportunity for investors but an opportunity for seniors to access critical services and for kids to get braces who couldn't afford them.

As I learned through these experiences, only after you have defined your purpose will you be able to clearly identify your path forward. Once you've done that, your decisions become simple and your life becomes more rewarding, as you know you are being true to yourself.

As you think about the things that are important to you, how can you refine those things to better understand what your purpose in life is? Are you present in your daily interactions? Are you optimistic about your future? *Are you fine or are you fulfilled?* Once you answer these questions, your decisions will become more defined and your goals more tailored to what is most important to you.

STOP HITTING SNOOZE

CHAPTER 2—WHAT IS HAPPINESS AND HOW DO WE ACHIEVE IT?

We all deserve to be happy, but we don't always know how to get there:

> Does happiness come from the possessions we have? No.
> Does happiness come from the amount of money we have? No.
> Does happiness come from things like alcohol and drugs? No.
> Does happiness come from our image or spouse? Not really.

I believe that while some of these external things can provide temporary joy, long-term happiness comes from a singular place: *within*. So, how does one go about achieving a positive self-image and achieving their highest level of happiness? It all comes down to balance.

It is critical to maintain balance in all areas of life to

ensure sustained fulfillment, as lack of balance can lead to unhappiness. And if you spend too much time in one area of your life, you risk becoming unbalanced (and thus, unhappy). There are several keys to personal happiness, which I define as how we feel about ourselves.

My "pillars" of balance are simple and consist of five key areas: family, friends, fitness (physical and mental well-being), faith and career (for the most part in that order). It is also important to keep balance among these pillars. While I love spending time with family, if I spend *all* my time with my family, I neglect the other areas of my life such as friendships, career and personal well-being. If I spend too much time on my career, I might miss important milestones with my kids. If I never work on myself, I will not be able to achieve the best version of myself to dedicate to my family, work and friends.

For many successful people, balance starts with faith, which can mean many different things—whether believing in a certain religion or worshiping a certain god. For me, faith means something different: that everything will work out for the best if we maintain the right mindset. To me, faith means that my best days are always ahead of me and that times of great opportunity are right around the corner.

Faith means that I see the best in everyone, even if they are not always kind or they don't think and act the same way I do. Faith means that some things in life are too difficult for the human brain to comprehend—and that there are signs out there that some things in life may be more than coincidence.

I met Rod at the ReblDads conference in Necker

Island, and I consider him to be "Oklahoma cool" with his vanilla-blond mustache and lightly tinted glasses. The way he explained faith resonated with me. Like me, he considered himself spiritual but did not necessarily practice a particular religion. Rod mentioned that he kept getting various signs, and that there was a particular number that kept coming back to him: 11:11. In fact, he is writing a book about it that I don't want to spoil, but I'll share a small portion of what we talked about on Necker Island here:

> *Brant, the main thing is I see 11:11 frequently and often around coincidences and synchronicities. It started with déjà vu type moments and was followed by an old friend who had been living in India for many years texting me for dinner one night at 11:11.*
>
> *Sometime after that, I started meditating. One day, I was on vacation with my wife Erin, and we went to the pool. I wanted to find a quiet place to meditate, but Erin wanted to go to the other side of the pool near three women, which I reluctantly agreed to do.*
>
> *Shortly after, I sat in a grassy area near the pool and closed my eyes. This doesn't happen all the time, but on that day while I was meditating, I saw a light. I asked the light where I should go and immediately overheard one of the women suggesting her friend travel to India.*

I asked the light how I would get there, to which the lady immediately responded, 'It's easy to get there, you fly from JFK direct to New Delhi and you can fly business class and sleep.' I then asked the light where to go, at which point the lady suggested that her friend go to the Himalayas.

Upon Erin's insistence, Rod booked a flight and made his way to the Himalayas, where he ended up meditating with monks in the mountains. As he meditated, he envisioned writing a book about his experiences, inspired by a book he had read long before about Richard Branson.

Rod knew he wanted to meet Richard Branson someday, and when he returned home from the Himalayas, he received an invitation to the ReblDads conference on Necker Island, where Richard Branson lives. Rod accepted the invitation and decided to take a short walk to explore shortly after arriving.

He walked down a path that appeared to be heading towards the beach and turned to his right, only to find Richard Branson standing in front of him looking out at the water. Rod walked up and introduced himself, meeting the man he had seen in his meditation session just a short time before.

There were countless other examples and signs Rod shared with me (which I look forward to reading when his book is published), but most important is that his stories of signs and faith made sense to me. I no longer believe that everything is simply coincidence. I had two signs shortly after leaving Necker myself, while my head was spinning from not knowing where to start on all the ideas that had been shared.

In the airport on the way home, I was thinking about Rod's story. I had just enough time to eat on my layover, and decided on Chinese food. I sat down, ordered some lettuce wraps and paid a short time later. I took my fortune cookie with me, and I had an unusual feeling that I might get some sort of sign from opening it. I broke the cookie apart and read the following:

Your experiences this week will all make sense within the year.

A couple of days later, my daughter was begging me to go get Chick-Fil-A. I obliged her, and after I had completed my order, the person asked me for my name. I replied "Brant," which he repeated before I pulled ahead. When I got to the middle of the drive-through, they confirmed my order and I headed to the pick-up window.

The woman there repeated my order before asking, "This is for Branson, correct?" My daughter, knowing where I had just returned from, how inspiring it was and my story about Rod, looked at me with surprise. Nobody had ever called me Branson in my life! It was eerily coincidental after spending the last week with Sir Richard and picking his brain about all things business and life.

My point in mentioning all this is not to prove this or that belief. It's to point out that faith in something tends to be a trait of the most successful. I once heard a statistic that around 89 percent of those that are most successful are faithful, spiritual or in other ways believe in something that cannot be explained by the human mind. In trying to understand this more, I do believe it will lead to a more balanced, and thus better, perspective.

The Shrimplin/Saiia family

My family goes to Florida for a week most winters to spend time with my mom and dad, who are Nana and Grandpa to my kids. We also visit with Uncle Tom and his son, my cousin and partner Tom and his wife Rachel, my sister Sarah, my brother-in-law Matt and my dear nieces, Lauren and Natalie.

We make it a point to travel to see each other often, as we believe that a tight-knit family that stays close is a key driver of happiness. We also gather on holidays and regularly travel together. I still go bowling with my dad once a week in the winter, and we golf together when we can in the summer. Family is the best, and ours shows up for each other.

On one of those trips to Florida, I was standing in the mirror drying off after a swim when I turned sideways and caught my reflection. I suddenly realized I had not been taking care of myself as well as I could have been. Granted, it is easy to judge yourself after a week of eating everything in sight at age 44, but I knew then and there I would commit to a more regular fitness schedule when I returned home.

I wasn't terribly out of shape, but I had never been truly committed to being consistent about my own well-being. Much like faith, I had also heard that many of the top entrepreneurs in the world felt fitness was a key component of their routines and well-being, so I figured I had little to lose.

I started with the basics: two dumbbells, a workout bench and walking. I slowly incorporated running into my walks and gradually lifted heavier weights along the way. I could feel my body and mind slowly transforming, and the discipline alone brought me a great amount of joy. After 18 months of steady exercise three to four days a week, along with a healthier diet, I rewarded myself with a treadmill (which, to be fair, my wife had been requesting for some time). I also got a Tonal system for resistance training, which was a big step up from my Amazon dumbbells!

I am now two years into my new health regimen, and I can honestly say that it is a critical part of my happiness and well-being. Not only do I feel better physically, but it has also led to a better and more focused state of mind overall.

If you are not incorporating some type of exercise into your life, perhaps it is time to reconsider. You can start small—and you will be amazed by how it transforms your way of thinking.

We have all heard the saying if you are not growing, you're dying. Still, I don't necessarily think growth always needs to come through higher revenue or increased profit margins. Staying mentally fit is just as (if not more) important than staying physically fit.

The irony of me writing this book is that, for the 25 years or so before, I probably hadn't read more than one or two books. I had countless books recommended to me, but trying to read them always reminded me of my academic days, which were not my cup of tea. By and large, I did not enjoy the academic world, where I was forced to sit still, read and regurgitate.

I am pure ADD and cannot sit still even to this day—and I do not enjoy reading about topics I have zero interest in (which, as a child, was just about everything a teacher put in front of me). I never understood why traditional academia felt so force-fed, and I was always on a mission to prove it was not critical for success. As I often told my mom in grade school: "I will never have a boss and will own my own company anyway, so why does school matter?"

Since my mom was a high school counselor, as you can imagine, my protests did not go over well. Still, she persisted (thank you, Mom), and I am happy that I went to college and got my degree.

My avoidance of reading came to a head on my recent trip to Necker Island. There were several books mentioned, and as I was writing them down, I told myself I should actually *read* one of them this time.

When I got home, I decided to commit to this and asked each member of the group to suggest a book for me to read covering any topic that was influential to them in their life. I now have a goal of reading two books per month, and am well ahead of schedule. I am thoroughly enjoying each read and picking up a lot of great information along the way.

My point is this: It is never too late for personal growth, and it is important that we continue to push ourselves in that category. If nothing else, you will gain valuable insight about others that you would not otherwise have known. That perspective will serve you well, even if for now you do not know exactly why or how.

One of my recent reads was a book called *Strength to Strength* by the great Arthur Brooks. He made a point about a successful financial executive that resonated with me. In Brooks' words, this executive was tremendously successful on Wall Street. She had made a fortune and was highly respected. However, she was unhappy and had been for many years. Her marriage was unsatisfactory, she was drinking too much and her relationships with her college-aged children were satisfactory at best. She also realized she had very few true friends. She lived to work, and her identity was completely wrapped in that one area.

She knew that putting all her eggs into the basket of her career was making her unhappy, but she couldn't find a way to change things. Brooks asked her, "If you know that working obsessively is making you unhappy, why are you not trying to change that to improve your happiness?"

After thinking about the question, she responded, "Maybe I would prefer to be *special* rather than *happy*.

Anyone can do the things it takes to be happy—go on vacation and spend time with friends and family. But not everyone can accomplish great things."

It struck me immediately that her definition of happiness was flawed. Happiness is not simply going on vacation. Happiness is not simply spending time with your family. If you are only doing those two things, you will quickly become unfulfilled as you are not striving for balance in all areas and working on being great in each one. Only once you strive for balance and greatness in all categories will you feel truly fulfilled. Striving for balance in life seems so simple, but if we don't do it intentionally, it can be incredibly difficult. We must strive to achieve balance each day.

For example, I've restructured each of my days to be sure I'm checking all the relevant boxes as a way of becoming more balanced. This was tricky for me, as I do not really like structure. If each day is planned to a T, it leaves no room for surprises and every day becomes monotonous. Because of this, I have to make some adjustments for spontaneity—but in general, I try to stick to the following:

- On normal days when I'm home, I try to go to bed at a reasonable time. This allows me to get up a bit earlier and spend some time with my kids before they go to school.
- I then take some time to read, which allows me to focus on personal development and other people's perspectives.

- On days like today, I take time to work on my book, to jot a few things down that I believe could be helpful to others.
- After that, I work on my physical and mental well-being by marching downstairs to exercise and lose myself in thought.
- By 9:30am, I am ready to jump into my workday, spending time on various tasks that will help my business become stronger and help those that I work with.
- Later in the day, perhaps around 4 pm, I taper off work and am excited to go home and see my kids. My wife, Lindsay, is usually prepping dinner by that time, where I may jump in to assist or help my kids with their homework.
- We then sit down for a family dinner, where we have one of my favorite discussions: talking about our day. We each get the table for a few minutes, with one person talking about the joys and perhaps the pains that came along with their day. At some dinners, we choose a specific topic to discuss (communication, for example) and how we can all become better at it.
- After that, we may go our separate ways, play a game together, watch TV or read. If we feel like it, Lindsay and I sometimes head out to connect with friends (as I write today, we are headed to Chicago to celebrate a dear friend's birthday).

The point I'm trying to relay is that by having some form of balance each day in the areas that are most important, you will undoubtedly have more balance in your life.

Sometimes, I do not work out for several days in a row, and that is okay. Sometimes, if I'm working on an important work project, I may not get the best sleep or be able to get up early to read, reflect and see my kids before school, which is also okay. Still, I always try to come back to this daily balance eventually, as I know how critically important it is to my overall well-being and happiness.

The great Jimmy V, who was a legendary college basketball coach and an advocate for cancer later in life, spoke to balance when he gave his now famous speech at the ESPYs. While the main point of the speech was to never give up and never give in, he also spoke on daily reminders of how to do this and how to live a full day (or as I interpreted it, how to be balanced). When asked how he got through life, he gave the following advice:

> *Each day's the same to me. To me, there are three things we all should do every day. Number one is laugh. You should laugh every day. Number two is think. You should spend some time in thought. And number three is you should have your emotions moved to tears. If you laugh, think and cry, that's a full day. That's a heck of day. If you do that seven days a week, you're going to end up with something very special.*

Richard Branson discussed one of his keys to staying balanced on our trip to Necker Island, which was to make time for yourself every day. His goal is to spend three hours alone each day, working on himself—in the form of exercise, reading, writing, meditating or any other form of personal development. Here is someone that has started 400 companies, that could spend endless time "working," most likely on projects that *would* help to change the world, and he still advocates for personal time and balance in life.

Richard dishing advice to Tom and I on Necker Island

As the old saying goes, "No one ever regrets not having spent more time in the office." This was written by Bronnie Ware, whose work as a palliative caretaker put her at the bedsides of patients with just weeks left to live. She speaks of five key regrets, two of which are very relevant to living a life with balance.

The number one regret was wishing they'd had the courage to live a life true to themselves, as opposed to the life that others expected of them. It's a regret about not pursuing your dreams, and therefore having dreams that go unfulfilled.

If you ignore what you truly value in life and instead pursue a path that your surrounding everyday culture foists upon you, you risk having real regret when you reach the end of your days.[1]

The second regret, which happened to be tops among the male patients, was this: "I wish I had not worked so hard." As she writes, "All of the men I nursed deeply regretted spending so much of their lives on the treadmill of a work existence." Ware writes that women certainly had this regret too but points out her patients were from an older generation, when fewer women worked outside of the home.[2]

Her points to me are crystal clear and reinforce living a life of balance. If you are unbalanced or unfulfilled and not striving to change it, you will most certainly end up with regrets. Work is great—as long as you are working on being balanced and leading your life with purpose.

To accomplish these tasks, there is another dimension to happiness. Though it isn't necessarily a pillar in and of itself, it is still key to becoming balanced. That dimension is discipline. Discipline, to me, can be described as a small step in the right direction of striving for balance.

If you do not have the discipline to see your family, make time for your friends, think about your faith, take a few steps towards well-being or improve your career, it

---

1. Perkins, Bill. 2021. *Die with Zero: Getting All You Can from Your Money and Your Life.* Boston: Houghton Mifflin Harcourt.
2. Ibid.

will be very difficult to become balanced. Simply put, even small amounts of discipline make you feel good. You do not have to start big on this.

As I wrote in a letter to my college-aged niece:

Have some discipline—discipline has a huge influence on happiness. If you are floundering, set a goal and accomplish it. It doesn't have to be huge—it could be, "I'm going to run for three days straight," "I'm not going to miss class for a month," "I'm going to tell my parents I love them everyday before I go to school this week." When you set a goal and are disciplined enough to accomplish it, that will feel good, and you will be on your way to bigger and better goals and more happiness because you're in control of yourself.

Of equal importance as you make progress in these various areas: It is critical to celebrate your wins. I recently had a conversation with the ophthalmologist I mentioned earlier about this. She was so singularly focused on the next thing, the next accomplishment, the next level she thought she had to get to, that she never stopped to smell the roses with what she had already accomplished. Or, as I told her, she wasn't celebrating her wins.

She immediately understood this and realized what I was saying. She made the time to connect more with friends, booked a trip to Colorado and attempted snowboarding for the first time. For just a few days, she didn't worry about the practice, working out or her family. She just lived in the present, took time to celebrate her wins and was a better person for it.

Dan Sullivan, an inspirational life coach, has his own philosophy for celebrating wins as it pertains to working on ourselves and our families. Before Dan goes to sleep, he writes down three things that he was grateful for that day, or as he calls it, three specific "wins." This has allowed him to not only boost his gratitude but to simultaneously boost his confidence.[3]

In his book *Tiny Habits*, the Stanford behavior scientist Dr. B.J. Fogg explains that feeling good and feeling like you're making progress are essential to growth and happiness.[4] As Dan shares in his book, writing down or even thinking about your three wins daily is one the of the most effective ways to continually measure your positive progress. You feel like you are always winning and moving forward. It keeps you in a constant state of forward momentum and confidence.

Additionally, Dan would think about the three wins he wanted to achieve the next day to make the three wins for tomorrow just as important.

As he explains:

I would go to bed feeling good but excited about the next day. I would wake up the next morning excited. Then, that day, I'd go out and try to have those three wins. But oftentimes, what would

---

3. Sullivan, Dan. 2021. *Gap and the Gain*. S.L.: Hay House Business.
4. Fogg, B J. 2020. *Tiny Habits: The Small Changes That Change Everything*. S.L.: Houghton Mifflin Harcourt.

happen is I'd have wins that were bigger than the three I had imagined the night before.

And then I'd come home and have the same exercise. And what happens out of this exercise—and this has been going on for 15 years with me—is **I'm always winning.**

Regardless of whether there are any setbacks or there's any disappointments, or there's obstacles that I've run into during the day, it doesn't matter. At the end of the day, I have my three wins. Tomorrow, I'm going to have three wins. In a week, I'm going to have 21 wins.

After a while, a couple of things start to happen. First, people start to get very excited. They get very happy. But on the other hand, they realize that it is their saying so that gives meaning to their past and their future. And that's a phenomenal breakthrough to realize, that you're telling the story about your life. The story you've already lived. And the story you're going to live tomorrow. That ability can get stronger and stronger as you go on.

In addition to measuring your wins, it is also imperative that you measure your happiness against your goals and not against an ideal or against what external forces would make you believe are the most important things in life. "Your happiness as a person is dependent on what you measure yourself against and you should only measure yourself against yourself," which Dr. Benjamin Hardy pointed out when writing *The Gap and the Gain* with Dan Sullivan.[5]

Later in Sullivan and Hardy's book, they tell the story of a woman named Sandi McCoy. Sandi is someone who had to stop caring what other people thought of her. She had to learn how to define success for herself, measure her own progress and become self-determined.

It's been a long road for Sandi. Over the past six years, she has gone from being morbidly obese at 400 pounds to losing over 240 pounds. She has used her social media platform to authentically share the struggles she continues to deal with, even after four years of maintaining her weight loss.

She often has people criticize her photos, calling her fat and making fun of her excess skin. She's learned to ignore the haters. She's learned that she needs to define success and happiness for herself, because even after all those gains, she can still fall down by comparing her figure or weight against others.

As she said on her Instagram account:

There used to be a time where I based my success on what I thought others wanted from me. I felt like I was always letting everyone down. Especially when it came to losing weight. It wasn't until I decided to make a list of what I actually wanted in life that I was finally able to succeed on the goals I set for myself.

---

5. Sullivan, Dan. 2021. *Gap and the Gain*. S.L.: Hay House Business.

Today I traced my calories, cleaned the house, did my knee exercises, went for a walk and played some kick ball. To some people, this might not sound like a successful day, but to me it is. Success is measured by you. No one else can set your happy meter.

Sandi is right: you have to be the one who defines success for yourself. You determine what a "successful day" looks like for you.

Additionally, by working on the fitness component of being balanced, Sandi is working to reduce her *biological age*. Your biological age measures how old your body seems and feels, rather than simply being based on your chronological age.

For example, you could have two 50-year-olds who, based on standard life expectancy tables, would be assumed to live the same amount of time. However, if one of those 50-year-olds was very out of shape and the other took the time to regularly work out and eat well, their biological ages would most likely be different.

Although it's impossible to reduce our chronological age, it is possible to reverse our biological age. Through diet, fitness and other lifestyle changes, biological age results can be improved. Lifestyle factors greatly impact how your genes are ultimately expressed, and your habits can impact your biological age more than your genes do. By following a few healthy practices, you can decrease your biological age.

For example:

- Balanced diet
- Regular exercise
- Effective sleep habits
- Stress management
- Sociability and community

Dean Jackson is a marketing expert and entrepreneur. Twenty years ago, Dean had the aha moment that "seeking success" had an inherent problem: Using the phrase "I'll be successful when…" led us to chase the wrong forms of success that didn't actually lead to the life we wanted. Dean decided to flip the question to put success in the here and now by asking himself, "I know I'm being successful when…". He came up with 10 questions:[6]

1. I can wake up every day and ask, "What would I like to do today?"
2. My passive revenue exceeds my lifestyle needs.
3. I can live anywhere in the world I choose.
4. I'm working on projects that excite me and allow me to do my best work.
5. I can disappear for several months with no effect on my income.
6. There are no whiny people in my life.
7. I wear my watch for curiosity only.
8. I have no time obligations or deadlines.
9. I wear whatever I want all the time.
10. I can quit anytime.

---

6. Sullivan, Dan. 2021. *Gap and the Gain.* S.L.: Hay House Business.

This list reflects what Dean identifies as the things that define success, or happiness, in his world. His measuring stick is his own creation. As a result, he is not chasing success or happiness that is defined by others.

Like Dean Jackson with his "I know I'm being successful when" list, Lee Brower, a successful entrepreneur and gratitude expert whose teachings have been viewed by more than 100 million people, developed a list of six questions he uses as a filtering process for making high-quality decisions.

Here are Lee's six filtering questions, which also act as his personal success, or happiness, criteria:

1. Is this opportunity, person, expense, adventure, experience, relationship, commitment, aligned with my values? (If the answer to this first question is no, then Lee doesn't answer remaining five questions; if the answer is yes, he continues.)
2. Will this opportunity take advantage of my unique ability and make me even stronger? Will it lengthen my stride?
3. How will this opportunity benefit mankind? Is there a bigger cause or purpose that will benefit society?
4. Does this make sense financially?
5. Is this transactional or transformational? In other words, is this a standalone opportunity or a gateway opportunity?
6. If I say yes to this opportunity, what then must I say no to?

As with Dean's criteria, these are Lee's own personal criteria for making decisions for the sake of happiness. The point isn't to adopt Dean's or Lee's or my personal criteria, although you can draw from them or steal them if you're inspired. Rather, the purpose of providing these lists is to get you thinking deeply about your own measurements.

So, there you have it: Keeping all the pillars of family, friends, fitness (physical and mental well-being), faith and career in balance with discipline equals happiness. The goal is to strive for greatness in all, or to identify those pillars that make you happiest and to do the same thing. While this may seem impossible, if you start small in each area and commit to doing it, you will surprise yourself with how good you can get.

Where do you fall in each of these categories? Have you ever graded yourself? I suggest ranking each category from 1-10 to see where you are at. If you are not at least a 7/10 in each area, you know what you need to work on to achieve your full potential—and to become a happier person.

STOP HITTING SNOOZE

CHAPTER 3—LEAVING YOUR OLD IDENTITY BEHIND

Change is hard, but you cannot change anything by doing nothing.

However, when you embrace the uncertainty associated with change rather than fearing it, you will go on to reach goals that you never thought possible. Like a snake shedding its skin, we must make changes throughout life to start anew.

If you are bogged down by who you are, then you are destined to remain stuck. You may be lacking the mental space to think intentionally about who you could be, depriving yourself of necessary growth.

The scores on your balance test mentioned in the last chapter will show if you need a change. If you are excelling in one area but falling woefully short in others, start thinking about redistributing your time. Determine whether the things you are doing are bringing you sustained fulfillment and if not, change is in order. To do this, you will need to release the old you to create the new you.

I recently met with Shane, who has been a friend and client of mine for the past 12 years. Shane owns an aerospace machine shop, which helps the world connect by providing low-cost internet services via satellites. Shane started small with just a few clients and gradually expanded into providing important parts to some of the top corporations in the United States (including Starlink, a satellite constellation operated by SpaceX).

Shane realized that to expand his capabilities even further, he needed to partner with someone who could help connect him to the right people to make his mission a reality—enter Gopi, another entrepreneur. Gopi promised a couple of solutions which were attractive to Shane, one of which was the purchase of his company to form a new combined entity.

This would allow Shane, now in his 50s, to cash in on some of his life's work to become financially free. At his stage of life, this was very enticing. In addition, Shane would be part of the new entity, which in theory would go on to reach new heights and allow both Gopi and Shane to reach their full potential.

Step one in expanding their capabilities was to move into a larger building. This would allow for additional machines and increased output, which would in turn lead to more contracts to expand revenue and profitability.

Shane immediately found a new building, which was twice as big as the previous space and had the ability to expand. Shane started negotiations for leasing the building and began to imagine which machines would be best to fill it.

As Shane approached Gopi with plans for the new building and new machines, he was met with resistance. Gopi was already running several operations companies and was hesitant to invest his time, energy and resources into Shane's vision. This was very discouraging for Shane, who continued managing his customers while trying to convince Gopi that this was a good investment.

Shane carried on, encouraging his employees to continue doing their best work, all while trying to do right by his long-term customers with the limited equipment he had. While this effort was certainly noble, it was also tiring. While trying to convince Gopi of his vision while continuing to run machines and keep everything else afloat, Shane was quickly headed for burnout.

Shane knew this partnership wasn't working and that something had to change. He negotiated a deal to move forward without Gopi and brought in Bob, a minority partner in the business who had his own successful shop.

Shane agreed that if Bob helped to buy Gopi out, then he would have a business to pass along to his son. This appealed to Shane, as he felt they had a shared vision of creating something that would be sustainable for long-term growth. A deal was struck, Gopi was out, and Bob and Shane would be off and running—or so he thought.

After a year or so of working together, it became clear that Bob was not the partner Shane thought he would be. He wanted Shane to continue to work in the same shop with the same capacity constraints and model as before. At the same time, Bob pushed Shane to take on more business, which Shane knew they did not have the capability to deliver.

It was precisely at this moment that Shane and I met for lunch. After years of hoping for an expansion that never materialized, Shane was completely depleted. In fact, he had already been in that state when he joined forces with Gopi in the first place.

Shane realized that nobody cared about his business as much as he did. He had a great deal of compassion for his employees and his customers and did not want to let them down, but in the process, he had given away so much of himself that he had little left.

Why did Shane continue to stay? He had already achieved financial freedom, or something that we call "work optional" in our line of business. He had long desired to travel after only seeing the walls of his shop day in and day out for the past 30 years. The decisions Shane made had set him up to do exactly what he dreamed of doing, yet he wasn't acting on it. He continued to do the same thing while expecting a different result.

I asked Shane why he stayed, and the answer was very simple: it was all he had ever known and it was intertwined with his identity. He would go to the shop, work hard, help his employees and take care of his customers. All of this was admirable, but not at the great cost he was paying.

It was clear to me that Shane had to leave as soon as possible, and so I asked Shane about his purpose. He realized that he had not been thinking about his purpose, as he only had time to think about the overwhelming daily stresses of the machine shop.

I asked him about balance—was he satisfied with his relationship with his family, his friends and his personal well-being? Or was he spending so much time on his career that all other areas were being neglected? He admitted that he was failing in many of these areas, because so much of his time was spent on work.

After talking with him about some of the principles in this book, I could see a light bulb illuminating in Shane's mind. He wanted to live a purpose-driven life, spend more intentional quality time with his family, re-engage with his friends and, for the first time in a long time, focus on his mental and physical well-being.

To do this, Shane knew that he had to let go of his old identity and focus on building a new one. He had to relinquish the daily grind and focus on a new beginning with an intention of doing things a different way. I'm excited for Shane and for who he will become through his personal transformation.

I met Jayson—or his preferred name, J Lo—at the Rebl-Dads conference on Necker Island. As we headed to our breakout groups, we kicked off our sessions by sharing our backgrounds. I found J Lo as well as his personal story to be particularly interesting.

By his own admission, J Lo is a coach and mentor to many, but his true gift is listening, learning and sharing wisdom with others, all of which immediately resonated with me. It was important to me to spend more time with him, as all the advice he gave could not be captured in one or two conversations.

First of all, J Lo is constantly changing his identity. There were many pivotal moments in his life that required transformation, like losing a significant amount of weight, going through an early divorce and finding fulfillment through radical career changes.

So, how does someone as successful as J Lo make such life-altering decisions when his life is seemingly perfect? By doing one important thing: facing fears. I asked him to expand on what this meant to him, and with speed and confidence—two of his most notable traits—he responded, "I had to face the fear of failing and the fear of regret."

J Lo started his career at a large technology company in 2005. Ultimately, he grew into the role of executive and led one of the most pivotal departments at his firm, where he was responsible for company strategy and the 700+ employees within his division.

By all necessary measures, J Lo was living a life of complete success. He was financially independent, highly respected and able to truly make a difference for his company and employees. He was also something else, which was the one thing he was seeking to avoid most: *unfulfilled.*

J Lo seemingly had it all, but he realized that attaining the things he *thought* would make him happiest only left him wanting more. He then decided to have a conversation with his wife, his greatest confidante, about his feelings of dissatisfaction and desire to change. With her support, he walked away from his company to start anew.

While he was unsure of what this new chapter would look like, he faced his fears and felt excited for what could come. Around that same time, he was invited to attend an insurance conference with an old business associate. While he had never really considered a career in insurance, much less life insurance, he still decided to go. It ended up being a pivotal point in changing his identity—and while he was there, he read a book titled *Becoming Your Own Banker*.

I was puzzled. How could one go from an executive position at a technology company to something seemingly as dry as life insurance? J Lo immediately responded, "Brant, it just made perfect sense to me. You are providing care and comfort to others in the form of financial support in their time of greatest need." Life insurance to J Lo was not about simply selling a product; it was about helping a person's loved ones with a financial transition after the unthinkable had happened.

J Lo went all in and became the number one life insurance producer in Canada. He held onto this competitive top spot for nine years, enjoying what he was doing and leading his life with purpose.

In October 2018, while enjoying considerable success and making millions of dollars per year, he had a conversation with a very influential life coach who changed his way of thinking. Dan Sullivan, a strategic life coach for entrepreneurs who has authored books and mentored thousands, suggested that even though J Lo was experiencing great success, he would eventually hit a ceiling of capacity.

While J Lo was somewhat surprised by this, he trusted Dan and asked him specifically what he recommended. Dan responded, "J Lo, you need to turn your competitors into your customers, and you need to give up your insurance licenses." *You must be kidding me,* J Lo thought. *Here I am, the number one insurance producer in the country, and you're recommending I give up my insurance licenses?*

However, the more J Lo thought about it, the more he realized that Dan was right. If J Lo was going to become truly fulfilled, he needed to share the wisdom he had gained. A change of identity was again in order, and in 2019, J Lo set out to start his own company, Ascendant Financial Inc. Initially, J Lo did not give up his insurance licenses; he needed to get the company off the ground first.

Having said that, he was committed to mentoring others and quickly assembled a talented team of producers. Some of his mentees had great success and others simply needed the right coaching to become million-dollar producers. Fast forward to 2024 and J Lo estimates that he will have gone from generating 100 percent of firm revenue himself to something closer to five percent, all while doubling overall revenue nearly every year from 2019.

I wanted to dig in more. By my accounting, J Lo had changed his identity no less than four times, two personally and two professionally, in a very short amount of time. As such, I asked him to share some tips on how to go from one identity to the next.

First, he told me it was always important to him to build a future that was bigger than his past. J Lo is a firm believer that our future is our property and that we have the power to make it anything we want. However, to properly create our future, we must sit down and visualize how it will look. Along with that, we must set a timeframe for when to put our changes into motion, and we cannot be vague. We must be specific, and we must have a timeframe.

As Dan pointed out, you can make massive progress

every 90 days. Breaking down your goals into 90-day increments is good for focus and motivation. By breaking goals down into smaller steps, you can focus more directly on what is right in front of you. You can make tangible and short-term progress, then look back and measure it to give yourself a sense of momentum.[1]

I asked J Lo for an example of this and he brought up his recent weight transformation. He said that in 2022, he woke up one day, looked in the mirror and realized that he did not like what he saw. He was 260 pounds, and while he was taller than most, he was still carrying around more weight than he wanted to.

He set a specific goal of weighing 223 pounds by the end of 2023, adding that he still didn't know how he would do it. Even so, his specific goal and timeframe was something he could easily wrap his brain around.

In addition, he did not worry about the specifics. He took a lesson from Dan, who suggested finding an expert to help get him started. Sullivan's strategy is to find a "who" instead of a "how", as discussed in his and Dr. Benjamin Hardy's book, *Who Not How*.

By setting a specific goal and finding a trainer, J Lo succeeded in his goal of getting his weight down to 223 pounds by the end of 2023. He proudly weighs a comfortable 216 pounds just a month into 2024. I wanted to learn more—what were the other things that helped him to transform his identity time and time again?

---

1. Sullivan, Dan. 2021. *Gap and the Gain*. S.L.: Hay House Business.

J Lo explained:

> *I had to lean into the things that bring me energy and to get rid of the things that drained me. Not only that, but I also had to be disciplined. There are days when I do not necessarily feel like working out. However, I give myself a five second countdown and then get to work, often discovering that those end up being my best sessions.*

By facing his fears, visualizing his future, setting specific goals, leaning into what brings him energy and staying disciplined in his pursuits, J Lo has successfully transformed his identity many times over. By his own admission, he could walk away from all his various businesses at any point in time, knowing that his investments can carry on without him. He can continue to mentor, stay present, remain in balance and live a future that is bigger than his past.

Creating a new identity is hard, to put it mildly. However, if you are to change and become the happy, fulfilled person that everyone strives to be, you will most likely have to change your identity multiple times throughout your life.

As you start to do this, you will have fears, which is only natural. You will also have to tune out the noise, including anything that prevents you from moving away from your old identity.

The greatest noise of all is self-doubt:

> *What if I can't do it?*
> *What if I fail?*
> *What if I don't like the new person I am becoming?*
> *What if I'm not as good at the new thing as I was at the old thing?*
> *What if I miss what I'm doing now?*

The answer to these questions is simple:

> *If you only focus on the what ifs of right now, you will never create a newer, better version of you.*

Noise also comes in the form of outside pressure:

> *How will my family and friends perceive this change?*
> *How will my employees/coworkers perceive this change?*
> *How will the people at my church perceive this change?*

If you focus too much on these questions, you will become stuck and never become the person you were destined to be. If there are people you lose in your life to become a more productive, better you, those are people who shouldn't have been in your life in the first place.

If you are happy and well, you can help others become happy and well. Most importantly, if you are seeking a new identity to help yourself and others, your family, friends, employees, colleagues and church will all support that change.

Do not underestimate the risk of inaction. Staying the course instead of making bold moves feels safe, but consider what you stand to lose: the life you *could* have lived if you had mustered the courage to be bolder.[2]

Why walk the path of creating this new identity? Why make these changes when the path of least resistance is to simply stay the course?

First, you want to avoid crossing the "line of despair," which is what I call burnout. Burnout means that you are lost. You may have success and appear to be just fine, but deep down, you know that you are floundering. Crossing the line of despair means that you are not helping yourself, which makes it impossible to help others. Crossing the line of despair means you have no plan, and you are stuck in a black hole. In summary: crossing the line of despair sucks.

You should strive to always be in the "ideal zone." In contrast to the line of despair, the ideal zone is one where you have purpose. The ideal zone is where you have balance and are happy, even-tempered and eager to teach others how to get to where you are.

Now, it's okay to fall out of the ideal zone at times; this often happens when we are shedding our old identity and creating a new one. I call this area the "fluctuation zone," which is a normal part of the process of change. It simply means that you are *temporarily* unbalanced and less than completely fulfilled, but you are not stuck there.

---

2. Perkins, Bill. *Die with Zero: Getting all you can from your money and your life.* Boston: Mariner Books / Houghton Mifflin Harcourt, 2021.

You might spend considerable time in the fluctuation zone. Just be aware that if you do not act while in the fluctuation zone, the line of despair awaits, and it is not a line worth crossing.

As I mentioned above, there are a few key things that will help you to make this transformation. Number one: give yourself grace along the way. We are all too hard on ourselves and accepting imperfection and learning from your mistakes are huge steps in making progress.

> Do you have to be perfect while on this path? No.
> Do friends expect perfection? No.
> Does family? No.
> Does the universe? No.

If the answer is "no" to all these questions, then why would we hold ourselves to an impossible standard? Worry about what you can focus on and what you can control, which does not equal perfection.

Mick and Caskey Ebeling, founders of Not Impossible Labs, a company designed to change the world through a potent mix of technology and story, give themselves grace in the form of their own ritual vocabulary. One acronym they use when someone is taking themselves too seriously is DOTYSOFUS. As they explain, it stands for "Don't take yourself so f****** seriously!" Remember: nobody is perfect.[3]

Another key aspect of making this change is being intentional with your plan. If you are being intentional,

---

3. Oelwang, Jean. *Partnering*. Optimism Press, 2022.

you are holding yourself accountable. Old habits are hard to break, and if we are not intentional about our actions and holding ourselves accountable, how will we ever be able to change?

Examples of being accountable could involve telling a close friend about your plan and then promising to report back about your progress. In the case of a friend of mine who went through a divorce, I helped him create a 12-month plan. That plan included recurring check-ins and texts to see how he was doing. It also involved quarterly dinners, where we would get together, talk about his progress and see how his transformation was going. Finally, we set a goal one year out: a trip together to celebrate his progress and further discuss his new family enterprise.

There are many ways to hold yourself accountable, and you will notice that each goal set and achieved will start to feel like transformation. You will realize that your newfound discipline to reach your goals makes you feel stronger and more confident.

To truly transform into a new identity, you must focus on balance and your effort to be great in many different areas. This may include a new set of goals.

For my client Shane, he needed to let go of all he had ever known and face the prospects of introspection and personal growth, something he hadn't truly pursued for decades. In the case of J Lo, he had to move beyond being the best on his own and focus on helping others become their best.

As you think about these things, ask yourself: Are you satisfied with your current identity? What can you change to create a new identity that is more fulfilling and more productive that will allow you to help yourself and others in new ways? Are you truly happy and satisfied with the current version of yourself, or do you need to rework your identity to better fit what's most important to you going forward?

CHAPTER 4—THE FORCE OF FRIENDS

There have been countless studies about the common traits of those who live the longest, most fulfilling lives.While there are many factors at work, there is one common thread that continues to ring true, which is the importance of friendships and community.

I've been blessed to have some very good friends throughout my life and remain connected to my original best friends, Mike, Ryan and Garrett, who I met in grade school. If you keep a close community of friends, you will never be alone, regardless of whatever you happen to be going through.

BRANT SHRIMPLIN

With middle school friends Mike and Ryan

With high school friend Garrett

Is it okay or normal to fall down from time to time? Of course it is. We all struggle in life sometimes, and it's during these times that we need friends the most—to help lift us up and get us back on track. This was the case that day I rushed to the hospital to meet my friend Scott.

Scott Matzka was a former pro hockey player and delivered the winning assist for the University of Michigan for a national championship in 1998. After a successful career overseas, he moved back to Michigan and married Catie, a close friend of my wife Lindsay for over 20 years.

Scott (bottom right) winning the NCAA National Championship at U of M

Scott and I became fast friends, constantly competing at the things I knew I had a chance at (like golf, pool, darts, ping-pong and so on). I was smart enough to avoid challenging a former pro athlete to anything overly athletic, and he was humble enough to know competing with me in a race wouldn't be too rewarding!

Scott had been privately expressing for some time that he was having issues with muscle pain and had recently had his hand lock up when he was working on a project in his garage. I'll never forget the day he told me this, as we were at a local lake with our kids, who happen to be the same gender and nearly the exact same age, with our girls being the oldest and our sons the youngest.

"Brant," he said, "I've been researching these symptoms I've been having, and I keep coming back to the same thing. It's been about nine months now, and everything is pointing towards something called ALS." Admittedly, I was not that familiar with ALS or its most common symptoms, but I inherently knew by the look on his face that it wasn't good.

For months, nobody knew about Scott's illness, as it is extremely hard to diagnose. There is no test for ALS; the only way you get a diagnosis is by ruling out several other diseases, which takes time and effort. Furthermore, you must go through a battery of physical exams, each designed to determine if your body is showing gradual signs of decline. It's a dreadful way to figure out a diagnosis and can take months to fully understand. I felt grateful that Scott and Catie wanted me to be a part of their journey so I could take notes, research some studies and ask the doctors questions, which would better allow them to focus on each other and their kids.

After a full day of testing, one of several that we had traveled to University of Michigan hospital to complete, Scott, Catie and I were moved into a room to wait for Dr.

Ava Feldman to come in. Dr. Feldman is a world-renowned researcher at the U of M and a world-class person. She is often doing research rather than seeing patients, but because of Scott's former ties to the school and his unique case (as a healthy young person, which is somewhat unusual for ALS), Dr. Feldman became his doctor and point person for treatment.

The room was silent as we waited for her to visit, not knowing what she would tell us. She came into the room with an associate doctor, sat across from us and started talking. After reviewing Scott's results and discussing his decline over the past several months, she delivered the heartbreaking news.

"Scott, it is my professional opinion that you have probable ALS," she said. "Unfortunately, there is nothing I can tell you other than to leave this hospital and live your life to the fullest. There is no way for me to know how long you will live, and there is no playbook for this part of your journey. In fact, this is the part of the process I hate the most, as there is really nothing else I can say or do. There are ongoing studies we will notify you about and that you can apply for, but there is no guarantee you will get into those studies or if you will be in the placebo group or receiving medication that could help prolong your life. I am very sorry to have to deliver this news, and I encourage you to surround yourself with those you love and to continue to lean on them for support."

We knew it was likely that we'd be getting this news, but actually hearing those words from one of the most respected doctors in the world was devastating. Scott mentioned his son Owen was only three years old and his daughter Reese, only seven. Even if he lived to the far end of his three-to-five-year diagnosis, it would still be far too little time to spend with his children.

"Brant, even if I live five years, Owen will only be eight," Scott said. "If I'm very lucky, perhaps he will be ten. Reese will only be twelve, and I won't be able to see her go to prom, much less be able to walk her down the aisle at her wedding. Not only that, but I may also only have another four or five hundred days to live. I need to think about how I'm going to live my life to the fullest from here on out."

The Matzka family

What happened next was truly remarkable. Every community that Scott had ever touched reached out with support and encouragement. The hockey community is a strong one, and many teams, coaches and former players reached out to offer help in any way they could.

Our local group of friends, coined the Texas Corners crew, rallied around Scott and his family to participate in raising awareness, helping with tasks around the house and filling in for Catie so she could continue to be the best parent possible to Reese and Owen.

Scott formed My Turn, a foundation that was born out of his idea to carry the torch for those who were struggling with this disease. This foundation needed help to launch, so our close group of friends formed a board. We clearly defined what the purpose of the foundation would be and worked with a media group to spread the message.

The My Turn boardroom

The Matzka family and friends

Scott shared his story at TEDx, which remains one of the most powerful speeches I have ever heard. He became an inspiration for those struggling with ALS who did not have his strength and reach. More than anything, he lived every day with purpose, spending real quality time with his kids, his wife and the countless friends and strangers whose lives he touched along the way.

Later, Scott needed help with everything from dressing to bathing to getting around. When he was no longer able to use his hands, he even needed help eating, and eventually, eating was replaced with a feeding tube. Catie did everything she could to assist him, but without a close group of friends who were willing to donate a significant amount of time, energy and resources, it would have been impossible for Scott and Catie to be with Reese and Owen as much as they deserved and wanted to be.

STOP HITTING SNOOZE

Scott and Catie at hospice

The Matzka family

Scott's force of friends remained with him until the very end. In his final days, when he could no longer stay at home and had to be moved to hospice care, he insisted that all his friends come with him. His family was kind enough to allow us to share these final moments together.

Scott with friends at hospice

A hospice facility is typically a place of great mourning where things are quiet and somber. Scott's experience was very different. He did not want us to mourn; instead, he wanted to celebrate his life until the very end. He wanted music, lively conversations, laughter and for us to enjoy our time together as we always had. We had no less than 30 or 40 close friends at his facility around the clock with as many of us in his room as could fit and an overflow crowd lining the hallway. Periodically, we cleared the room so each of us could talk to Scott one on one.

Typically, we are not able to sit down with our dying loved ones to tell them how important they are to us, that we appreciate the many lessons they taught us or how courageously they are fighting a terrible disease in the most gracious way possible.

When Scott took his final breath, Catie was lying in his bed holding him and 10 of his closest friends and family were in the room. Scott had said his final goodbyes to Reese and Owen, who were also close by. Scott's force of friends was there for him when he left, and they remain there for Catie to this day.

This journey with Scott turned out to be four years of some of the best, most rewarding and most difficult times of my life, the entirety of which could make up a separate book. Scott passed away in December of 2018, but I will always remember my times with him and the lessons he taught me along the way.

With help from caring, dedicated friends, Scott was able to dictate how the last four years of his life would play out. With his personal force of friends, he created a journey for himself that touched many other lives, including mine, and ultimately made a tremendous impact. Without those close-knit friendships that were fostered and nurtured over time, the overall experience for his family would have been very different.

During Scott's journey, there was also a time that I needed my force of friends to help me, which happened to coincide with the very day that he was diagnosed. His post-diagnosis dinner and attempt to decompress ran long, and I was late for a fantasy football league draft. I showed up around an hour late to the draft party at my own house, unable to let anyone know why. My friends were excited to get started and gave me an appropriate amount of ribbing for showing up late to my own league. As I tried to gather myself after a very difficult day, my phone rang. I looked down and noticed it was a call from my dad, which was somewhat unusual at that time of the evening. I answered and he started right in.

"Hi buddy," he said. "How are you doing? How did things go at the hospital today?"

"It was hard, Dad," I said. "Scott was officially diagnosed with ALS. He has a long road in front of him. I'm exhausted and I have ten of my best friends in the basement ready to get started with this fantasy football draft. I'm trying to compose myself and head down there."

"Well, I'm proud of you for going and being there for them," my dad replied. "I know how much he appreciates your help, and for that, you should be very proud. Brant, I hate to be the bearer of bad news, particularly on a day like today, but you know how I haven't been feeling quite right as of late?" Naturally, my heart sank into my stomach.

"Yes Dad, I know. What's going on?"

"Well, your mother and I went to the doctor today, and unfortunately, I was diagnosed with Parkinson's disease."

Those words hit me like a ton of bricks. Two of the most important people in my life found out on the very same day that they were carrying terrible diseases, one fatal and one life-altering. I now had two missions: to support both my dad and Scott in any way I could.

I continued to help take Scott to his respective appointments, while also trying to learn as much as I could about Parkinson's disease. While I knew I could have some impact, it was clear they would need more support than I could give on my own. This is when a force of friends shows up, such as David and Jon, who immediately stepped in to help the Matzka family from the beginning.

With friends Jon (left) and Dave (middle)

I had friends like Mike, my OG, who lives just a few doors down from my folks and who offered his assistance with various responsibilities for my dad, which has been appreciated more than he will ever know. Without my personal force of friends, I would not have had the same amount of impact nor the support I needed to get through these difficult times.

A newer friend of mine, Mike, was going through a divorce a couple of years ago. Understandably, he was in a tough spot trying to figure out how his future would look. He was a successful doctor, had two children in middle school and was active in his church.

Going through a divorce is a painful process that requires a complete rewiring of many aspects of life. It requires pivoting from an old identity to a new identity, which requires not only a new way of thinking, but support from those close to you who can help you crystallize a path forward. Mike was floundering. He wasn't sure how this news would be received by his family, friends, church and children or how he would be perceived. Luckily, Mike had two friends that came to his side.

One was our close friend Kevin, who immediately stepped up to help. Fortunately, Kevin is the type of person who would do anything for you and would not let someone close to him fall down. The other one was me, a newer friend, but one that also felt compelled to help. I sat down one morning and wrote out ideas that would lead to a positive path forward, and the three of us met for dinner that evening and discussed the plan. We talked about building Mike's new identity and purpose and how to find the real keys to happiness. We discussed tuning out any external noise and creating a new family enterprise, surrounded by the love from his daughters, friends and family.

Mike came away from that dinner with a new outlook on life. As he has mentioned countless times since, his path forward would not have been as easy or accelerated without the power of his friends who were behind him. As we told Mike that evening, "We are always here as friends for you—just dare us not to be."

Today, Mike is in a great place and often references how the concepts we discussed were a big wakeup call that allowed him to transform his way of thinking. I'll always be grateful for that experience, how our small part was able to help him and for the inspiration it gave me to write this book.

With friend Mike (left), with friend Kevin (right)

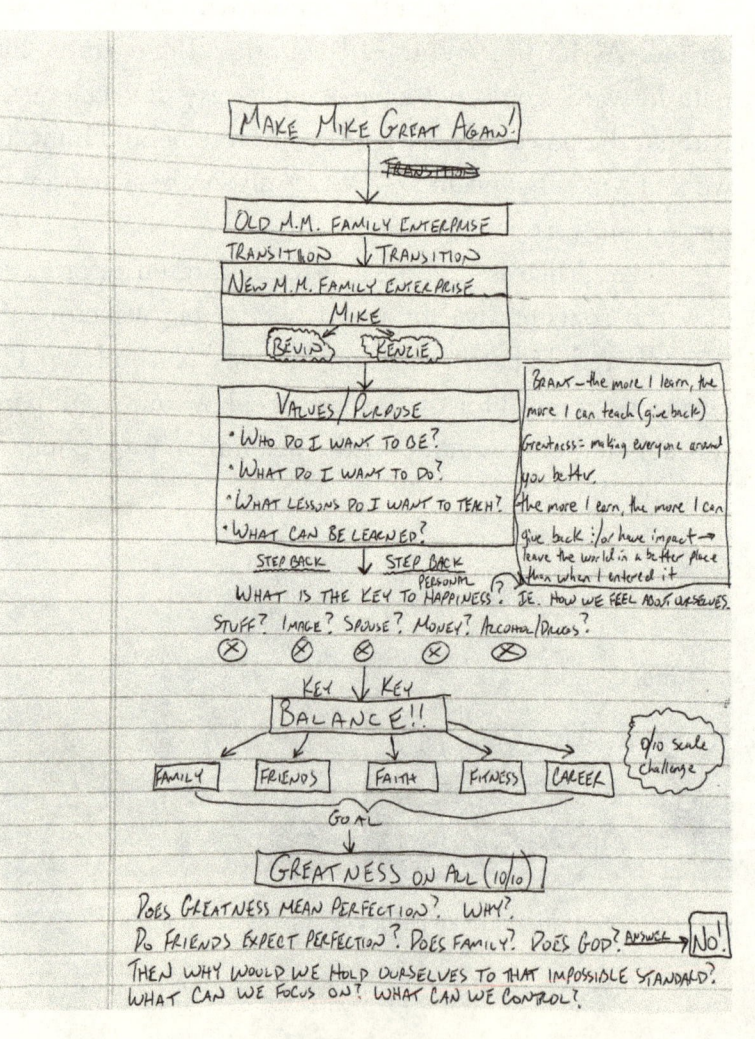

The Mike action plan

STOP HITTING SNOOZE

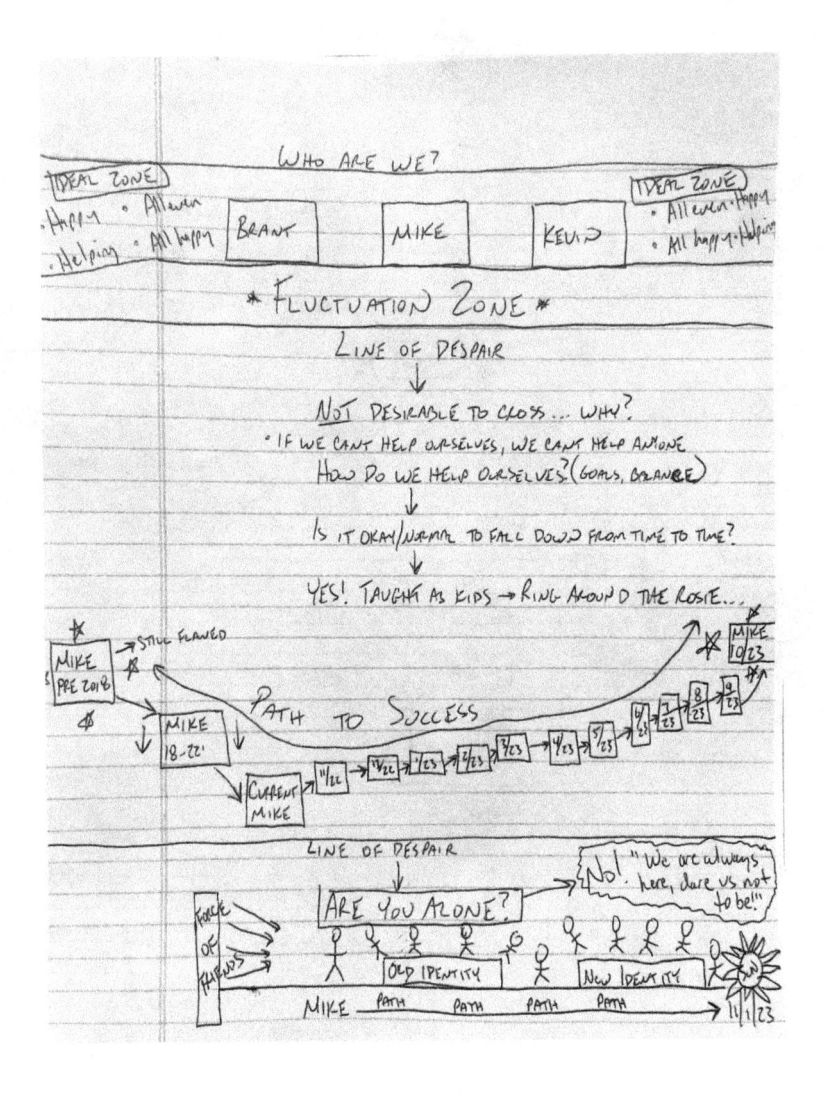

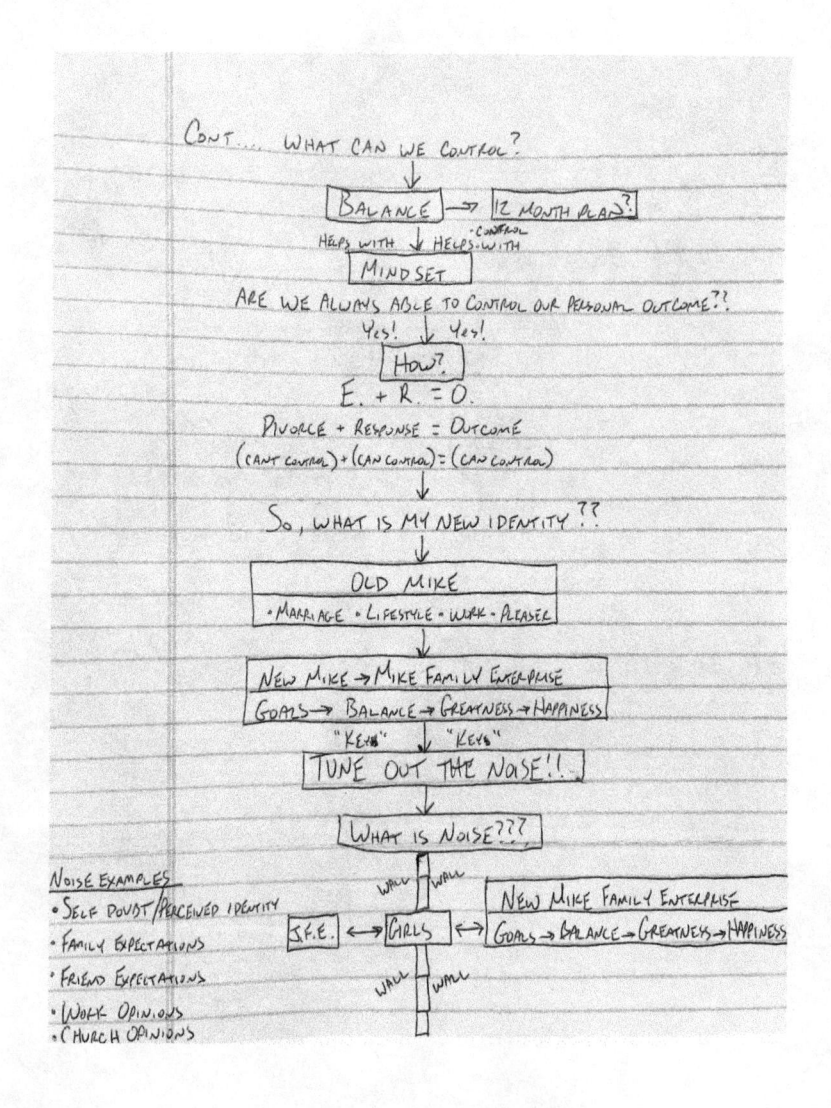

Cont... WHAT CAN WE CONTROL?
↓
BALANCE → 12 MONTH PLAN?
HELPS WITH ↓ HELPS WITH · CONTROL
MINDSET

ARE WE ALWAYS ABLE TO CONTROL OUR PERSONAL OUTCOME??
Yes! ↓ Yes!
How?
E. + R. = O.
DIVORCE + RESPONSE = OUTCOME
(CAN'T CONTROL) + (CAN CONTROL) = (CAN CONTROL)
↓
SO, WHAT IS MY NEW IDENTITY??
↓
OLD MIKE
• MARRIAGE • LIFESTYLE • WORK • PLEASER

NEW MIKE → MIKE FAMILY ENTERPRISE
GOALS → BALANCE → GREATNESS → HAPPINESS
"KEYS" ↓ "KEYS"
TUNE OUT THE NOISE!!
↓
WHAT IS NOISE???

NOISE EXAMPLES
• SELF DOUBT / PERCEIVED IDENTITY
• FAMILY EXPECTATIONS
• FRIEND EXPECTATIONS
• WORK OPINIONS
• CHURCH OPINIONS

WALL WALL
S.F.E. ↔ GIRLS ↔ NEW MIKE FAMILY ENTERPRISE
GOALS → BALANCE → GREATNESS → HAPPINESS
WALL WALL

STOP HITTING SNOOZE

WHY WALK THIS PATH?

- AVOID CROSSING THE LINE OF DESPAIR
- FEELS BAD TO HAVE NO PLAN (BLACK HOLE ●)
- WE BELIEVE IN YOU, SO WHY SHOULDN'T YOU?
- IF YOU'RE NOT RIGHT, WE'RE NOT RIGHT
- YOUR TURN NOW, OUR TURN LATER (EQUITY IN EACH OTHER)
  IE → WE ARE ALL INTERCONNECTED
- TO GET BALANCED, BE WELL

KEYS | KEYS
↓

GIVE YOURSELF GRACE!!!

BE INTENTIONAL!! (OLD HABITS ARE HARD TO BREAK)

BE ACCOUNTABLE!!

Recurring check ins	Quarterly dinners	One year celebration if warranted
	1/2023	11/1/23
	4/2023	
	7/2023	

12 MONTH PLAN Q'S
WHERE DO I FOCUS FIRST?
DO I REALLY NEED ALL THE THINGS I HAVE?
DOES IT REALLY MATTER WHAT EVERYONE THINKS?
IS TODAY/NORMAL TO CHANGE?

LIFE IS SHORT : THERE IS NO TIME TO WASTE

My force of friends concept was later tested again in my business. Tom and I had always had a vision of combining companies, which became a reality on the morning of February 22, 2018.

Tom had notified his former company that he was jumping ship, and we celebrated our first day of working together. Shortly after his team arrived at the office post announcement, we got a call from our mutual friend Chris, who was clearly distraught and was struggling to get his words out.

"Brant, I just found out that Adam suffered from sudden cardiac arrest last night and unfortunately it does not look good," he said. "Will you say a prayer for him and let Tom and some of our other friends know? We need to pull together and do everything we can to help."

Adam was a vibrant, handsome, 38-year-old marathon runner with more ambition than most of us will ever hope to have. He was a successful attorney who owned a law practice. He was our close friend, and he also provided critical legal advice for our various companies.

STOP HITTING SNOOZE

Adam and Melissa

With friends in Northern Michigan

The last thing I expected to happen on our first day of working together was to get a devastating call about a close friend suffering a heart attack. Adam was struck while vacationing with his parents and two young children in Florida.

Our group of friends sprang into action. Adam's two best friends boarded the next flight to meet him, and soon Melissa was quickly surrounded by loved ones offering their help with everything from emotional support to childcare to finances. In just a couple of days, it was clear that Adam would not recover, and the difficult decision was made to let him go. Almost as quickly as we got the bad news, we lost Adam.

While devastating to go through, it was still undeniably uplifting to see how quickly his close friends rallied around him and his family. Had Adam not fostered and nurtured his relationships over time, it undoubtedly would have been much more difficult for his family to move forward. As tragic as it was to lose Adam, his life story was still a testament to how a strong force of friends can transform life for the better—for others as well as ourselves.

We all have equity in our friends, and they have equity in us. In my case, if something is not right with those closest to me, it is impossible for me to feel completely fulfilled. If someone is down, it only makes sense to help them, as your time of need will come eventually. All too often, I see people get married and allow their friendships to die. I also see people who regret letting this happen as they grow older and realize how lonely they are.

The good news is that it is never too late to develop your network of friends. Several of my closest relationships are with people that I met in adulthood. Had I not been open to meeting new people and taking the time to get to know them, my life would be much less full. No matter where we are in life, our friendships must be nurtured.

With friends Garrett (left), Mari (middle) and my wife Lindsay

With friends in Greece

With friends, celebrating in Las Vegas

My wife Lindsay and I made a point to nurture our friendships from the moment we were married. We decided that we each needed one day a week to spend with friends and that it was essentially non-negotiable: her day was Wednesday, my day was Thursday.

When the kids were young, and if it was our day to take care of them, we would step up and handle it—even if our kids had colds or were otherwise feeling lousy. If either of us had a long day at work, came home and simply wanted to relax but it was our day to take care of the kids, guess what? We didn't relax. We made dinner for the kids, played with them, changed diapers and read them bedtime stories. Then, oftentimes, once the other spouse got home and wanted to talk when it was time to finally relax, we talked. While it was sometimes hard to do, we did not let the seasons of our life get in the way of keeping our friendships strong.

Who makes up your force of friends? Are you nurturing your old friendships to keep them alive? Are you putting in the time now to meet the people who will eventually be there for you when times are tough? If not, how can you evolve? What steps can you take today to improve things going forward?

CHAPTER 5—YOU ALWAYS CONTROL THE OUTCOME

Regardless of what happens to you in life, you always have the ability to control the outcome. It is possible to turn each event, positive or negative, into something that is powerful, meaningful and useful. Just remember this time-tested formula:

Event (can't control) + Response (can control) = Outcome (can control)

$$E + R = O$$

Since we are able to control our response to any event, we can **always control the outcome.** You cannot always control the event, but you can control the outcome. **The key is your response.** You have the choice to let things linger or to let it go. Choose to let go. This is something that you can train yourself to do. Eventually, you will be able to consistently avoid negativity.

Most often, when others project their negative feelings onto you, they are making a mistake, and it's best to forgive them and move on. It could also be the case that their emotions are causing them to act out of character. Finally, it's also possible that someone is simply a bad person. Those people do exist and should be avoided.

You may naturally be thinking about events in your life where you could not control the outcome, such as the passing of a loved one from a terminal disease. You may be thinking about my friend Scott, who died from ALS and was not able to cure himself.

While it is true that his outcome was set, the way he responded to that event changed the way he viewed living and dying. His reaction to ALS was not to sit around waiting to die but to continually connect, and to share and raise awareness of the disease. He dramatically changed the path that he took and thus changed the outcome of his diagnosis.

The last four years of Scott's life were filled with more profound moments of connection with everyone he encountered than he'd had in the prior 36. He smelled the roses, engaged with his children in ways that he hadn't before and made the most of every moment. He lived to make every single day count and lived his last four years in ways that would have taken more than a lifetime had he not been diagnosed with ALS.

Scott responded to his prognosis in a way that allowed him to control the outcome of his disease while knowing it would eventually take his life. I chose to respond by actively assisting him and remaining a positive force for his family, and I will also be forever grateful for how my entire family responded to his diagnosis as well. We all die, so the fact that Scott was going to pass away at some point is not the moral of the story. It was how he lived, and how we all live in times of crisis, that matters most.

Scott and I had battled many times at golf and had often talked about the best tournament in the world, the Masters at Augusta National. So, one of the first things we did after his diagnosis was to take a bucket list trip to the Masters tournament at Augusta National. For anyone who golfs, this is sacred ground, and it was a place he had always wanted to see.

My Uncle Bill and Aunt Susan graciously hosted us, found us tickets to the tournament and provided several rounds of golf at a nearby course to be sure we had the best time possible. We spent the day walking the grounds, interacting and watching the players.

I vividly remember us sitting calmly near Amen Corner, a famous stretch of three holes where players can get tight as they have to hit over the water and land on a small, fast green—something that unnerves even the best golfers in the world.

In all, the trip was the best *response* we could have had, as was my family's gracious gesture of offering to host us, and it resulted in memories that we would always cherish.

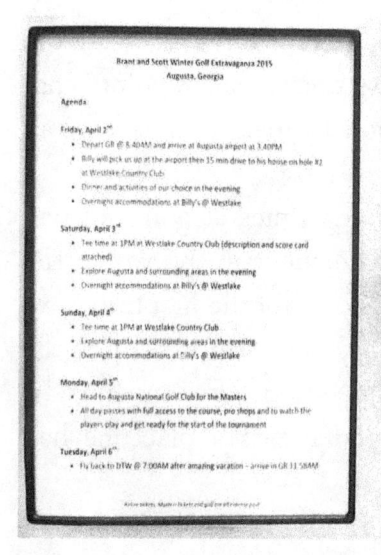

With Scott (left) and Uncle Bill (middle) in Augusta, Georgia

Controlling your response, especially in times of great stress, is very difficult to do. I have been practicing this theory for some time, and I still find myself reacting in negative ways from time to time. But through practice, my positive response times are becoming much faster. I do see a point in the future where my responses will become consistently positive.

I'll never forget the day I was fired. As far back as I can remember, I always had a job—starting with shoveling driveways as a kid and evolving into mowing lawns and later, corn de-tasseling, a painstaking summer job that involved picking the tassels off the top of corn stalks in 90-degree humidity. I quickly realized that physical labor was not my thing and started to get more creative about how I could make a buck.

After having mild success going door to door to sell my old children's books, I moved onto slinging gum at Portage Central Middle School. I would bike to Sam's Club, a bulk food store that carried packs of gum en masse, and buy gum to sell to my classmates.

As I sat in math class one day, most certainly daydreaming about anything but math, the vice principal showed up. He told me to come out into the hall with him. As we were on our walk, he asked, "So, Brant, do you know where I might be able to buy some gum?"

Needless to say, my business was shut down shortly after. I had to pivot to painting houses, working at a pharmacy and taking a job as a permanent dishwasher at our local Pizza Hut, despite their promise to promote me to server.

My career evolved over time, part of which was shaped by my parents. My dad worked in finance and my mom was a counselor at a local high school. My dad taught me three valuable lessons at a very young age: the power of a strong work ethic, to never limit myself and that equity was extremely important. My mom's lessons were equally as valuable: be persistent and never give up.

While I never imagined working with my dad, it eventually happened after the summer of 2002. I had taken several jobs in finance and was sure it was my path. I had an opportunity to work in the finance capital of the world, New York City, in 1999. After a short time there, I headed back to my hometown of Kalamazoo, MI, where my grandfather was suffering from congestive heart failure.

I expected to stay in Kalamazoo only to spend the last few months of my grandfather's life by his side, but it turned out that one of my summer roommates would become my future wife. We stayed in Michigan. After all, Kalamazoo is a great place to raise a family, and it was where we had a tremendous amount of support.

Working together with my dad started in November of 2002. He ran the insurance department of a nationwide broker dealer, a financial firm that employs various types of financial advisors. Originally, the plan was for me to be his on-the-ground employee that traveled across the country to help advisors with their client's insurance needs. However, only three months into the job, the CEO decided to move the department to New York. This left my dad without a corporate management position or a steady stream of income, forcing us to make a choice.

We could continue to work together and build something, or we could go our separate ways. As I wasn't quite refined in the Response part of the $E + R = O$ formula at this stage, my natural reaction was to cry—not exactly the best way to handle adversity and move forward. My dad reassured me all would be fine and that we should view the change as a chance to build a new financial services practice together.

We did this the hard way, by holding monthly seminars and sending out thousands of invitations with the hope that 30 to 40 people might show up. If we were able to get appointments with a few of them, we considered it a success. If one decided to work with us, we considered our efforts and money spent for each seminar a win.

I'll never forget the first clients we landed from these

seminars: Danny and Judy, who agreed to invest $85,000 with us. It was in or around late 2003, and the first account that we call "fee based" in our line of business, meaning one that would provide a steady stream of residual income over time if we provided great service.

By 2007, my dad and I had built what we considered to be a successful practice that provided a great standard of living for both of us. Around that time, two events happened that would test my evolution on $E + R = O$. The first was the stock market crash of 2008-2009, where the market lost 57 percent of its value. Not only that, but the housing market also fell roughly 30 percent, leaving clients panicking.

By this time (around age 30), I had learned to respond to negative events with a sense of calm. The worse the event, the calmer I became. If I could do that, it would provide reassurance to others in times of crisis. Our ability to remain unfazed helped us greatly, and we lost very few clients during the crash.

Around the same time, I started to express an interest in leaving corporate America to my dad. I wanted us to start our own private wealth management practice. I had always wanted to work for myself, and while we had great freedom within our current environment, we did not have *equity,* or ownership, in our practice. It was winter of 2009, coinciding with the lowest of lows for the stock market and the birth of Avery, my daughter.

We researched different companies we admired and could align with to start our own practice and decided that in the fall, we would make the jump. We had lots to do as we prepared to start a company, including choosing a company name, finding an office location, creating a website and branding materials and so on.

I pulled into the office on Friday, June 25th, tired from a sleepless night with my five-month-old daughter. I was ready for another day of work with my dad, who insisted that I get to the office at 7 am each day regardless of my lack of sleep! Shortly after discussing our responsibilities for the day, the branch manager came into our office and shut the door behind him.

An eerie feeling came over the room, like we were about to get sent to the principal's office because we did something wrong.

"I hate to have to deliver this news to you," he said, "but our CEO has found out that you are planning to leave—and as a result, you're fired!" After so many years at the company and helping them build their now sizable insurance department from scratch, my dad was stunned. He was 61 years old and had never been fired from a job in his life.

"You need to leave right now," the manager continued. "You cannot take anything with you other than your personal items, so you need to pack your things and leave." We packed up our stuff and walked out the door. Just like that, we were out of a job.

We were tipped off that letters were being prepared to go out to all our clients, notifying them that we were no longer employed at the company and that a new team of advisors would be taking over for us on Monday. I'll never forget my first call to my wife Lindsay as I left the office.

"Hi, honey," I said. "I have some bad news to tell you. My dad and I were just fired." As you can imagine, this wasn't the most welcome news after suffering a very stressful couple of years with the market crash and having a new baby at home.

Not only that, but it was no coincidence that they fired us on June 25th, right before we were scheduled to get our quarterly check. This left us with a big gap in our income and with nowhere to go.

Keep in mind that at that time, we had no office, no stationery, no website, no furniture and hadn't even finalized which company we were going to align with. In our business, we are not able to discuss where we are going until our advisory licenses change, meaning that until we aligned with a new custodian to hold our client assets, we were not able to disclose where we might go.

Understandably, there were many ways that we could have responded to this situation. A common response would have been to curl up in a ball and cry, like I had done earlier in my career. I refused to do this and instead viewed it as a challenge and a great opportunity.

We had a vision for our own business, and in my mind, that gave us a head start. It was also an opportunity for me to step up and *give back* to my dad by being a sturdy presence in the storm. At 61 years old, this sudden change was initially very jarring for him.

With what we knew was looming on Monday morning, I called our clients the day we were fired to tell them we had very exciting news. We were starting our own company, which we could not disclose to them yet, but we very much looked forward to sharing further details in the coming days. We told them we had always dreamed about taking this step, and now that we had, we hoped they would come on this journey with us.

Granted, it wasn't the best timing to call our clients with a big change. Many of their portfolios were down substantially after the stock market crash. They would also have to make a choice to trust a company they had never heard of.

Around this same time, my sister and brother-in-law came to town. They own a consulting company in Boston that helps companies to transform their businesses. Together, we huddled up in the family living room and began brainstorming a company name, which turned into a fun game with all kinds of names being thrown out for discussion.

We ruled out Shrimplin and Company, because we knew one day we'd want to expand and hire other financial advisors. At one point, Matt asked, "What is today's date?" Someone replied, "Six twenty-six," as it was 6/26 of 2009. "How about 626 Financial?" he said.

While the day before had been a difficult day, 6/26 represented a great new opportunity. It was the day that our dream of starting our own financial services business was finally coming to fruition. 626 Financial was born in our living room. Today, it has grown into a practice that manages hundreds of millions of dollars.

We retained approximately 98% of our fee-based clients, despite our uncertainty after being fired. This turned out to be a very poor decision for our former firm and a blessing in disguise for us.

In this time of great crisis, we chose to respond with excitement and a positive outlook. We took something that was very negative and turned it into a great opportunity. It was yet another life lesson: If you respond to unfortunate events with a positive mindset, you can control your outcome.

Some key things to think about: How are you responding to difficult events in your life? Do you view these events as an opportunity for positive change? Are you focused on a positive outcome or are you responding in a way that continually leads to a negative outcome? How can you change your perspective to view all events as an opportunity to grow?

CHAPTER 6—GIVE TO GIVE

Until I met Justin Breen, I did not fully understand the concept of giving to give. Breen came up with a framework for those that are the happiest, most evolved and most successful. Once his concept sunk in, I quickly realized that I had always led with a give-to-give mindset.

As Justin describes in his formula, there are essentially four types of people:

1. Those who get to get—people who reach out to thousands to attract their first five clients. You are doing tasks to get something in return.
2. Those who get to give—with these folks, they are perhaps thinking of giving, but mostly still thinking about getting something themselves.
3. Those who give to get—in this stage, you have begun the process of giving. However, you are still stuck on getting something in return.

4. Those who give to give—this is the highest level of personal evolution: freely giving and expecting nothing in return. There are no competitors, only collaborators. You are giving at will in order to learn, to teach others and to become a better person.

As I took some time to think about this, I realized that I had automatically done this throughout my life. In turn, I had received more back than I could have ever hoped for. It was always the rewarding feeling of giving to others that made me feel best.

There are many examples of giving to give. One example that stuck out to me was brought up at the Rebl-Dads conference when I met Adam Holt in Necker Island in one of my breakout sessions. We delved into the many things that helped to make him a successful entrepreneur and father. As I was writing this book, I asked him about the concept of giving to give, and he shared a story with me that resonated:

> *I came up with this phrase a while back that I call give 3x the value. For example, I had a friend who asked me for a referral, and I gave him three. He couldn't believe that I would go above and beyond what was asked. Going forward, this became the standard for me: to give 3x more than anyone else's expectations.*

Adam's concept was supported by a very successful financial advisor in Texas. The advisor shared that he was dealing with a great amount of stress. Naturally, Adam asked him how he best managed these challenges.

The advisor shared that whenever he was overwhelmed, annoyed, beat up or otherwise unhappy, he would call three people in his network and ask how he could help them. This redirected him back to his purpose. He also became addicted to supporting others.

Giving to give can be simple. I was recently in Chicago for work and popped into a CVS to pick up a razor. There was a customer standing in front of me at the register, a kid that was a bit disheveled with maybe 10 or so items wrapped in his arms—a Mountain Dew, a candy bar and a magazine are the few things that I remember. He set them down to begin his checkout and glanced back only to notice that I only had one item. I smiled and waited for him to check out, but he insisted that I jump ahead of him despite being ready to scan his first item.

I thanked him, walked around and got my razor scanned. I then asked the employee to scan all his items, as I wanted to pay for them. It couldn't have been more than $15, but his reaction was priceless.

"You're kidding me, you would do that for me!?" he asked incredulously. "I can't believe this! Nobody has ever done anything like this for me before! Wow, you are so nice!" The employee softly said, "You do something nice for someone and they do something nice for you." I felt great walking out of that store—we had both benefited from a give-to-give situation.

If you are feeling discontent, giving to give is the quickest and easiest way to feel better about yourself. Much like the example of the successful financial advisor offering favors to friends, I have found that doing a kind act for others makes me feel good and makes everything else in life feel better.

It does not have to be something monetarily grand. A simple compliment or lending a helping hand is plenty. In fact, just listening to someone vent about their latest accomplishments or struggles can have a tremendous impact on them.

I was in Key West a few years back for a friend's 40th birthday weekend. The sun had come down, the music had gone up and there were many partygoers out and about enjoying themselves. My brother-in-law Matt and I took in the sights of the city and did our fair share of people watching.

Matt is a classic give-to-give type, mostly in the form of advice. He has a particular predilection for eccentric clothes, and on that evening, his flair for the dramatic came in the form of a colorful, graffiti scattered Versace sweatshirt.

As we approached The Smallest Bar in Key West, a 72-square foot outdoor bar that isn't much larger than your typical elevator, a gentleman took notice of Matt's sweatshirt. The gentleman seemed to be more of a local than the typical Key West tourist, standing near the bar without a beer or anything to occupy him. He kept commenting that he loved the colors and style of Matt's sweatshirt and asked him several questions about it.

We ordered beers and talked with this gentleman for a few minutes until Matt asked me to hold his drink. He pulled off his sweatshirt and handed it to this gentleman, who erupted with joy. He was shocked that someone would even consider doing this for him.

"Here you go, it's yours now," Matt said. "I hope you enjoy it as much as I have, and I hope you have a great rest of the night!" The man was elated, and you could tell that this sweatshirt meant the world to him—just a simple gesture of a hooded sweatshirt, albeit a very nice one.

"I have seen you do a lot of cool things in your life," I said to Matt, "but that was one of the coolest things I have ever seen you do." Matt gave to give and walked off in a pit-stained undershirt after proudly making somebody else's day.

Oftentimes, the greatest gift of all costs nothing. It is the gift of time. I know what you're thinking: time is often the one gift we can't freely give. There is work to get done, kids to parent, pets to take care of, spouses that need attention and many other things to gobble up our spare hours. However, once you let go of the unnecessary to start to make time for others, you will feel better and more relaxed. It's counterintuitive, but it's true.

This was true as it related to my time with Scott. Coming into that journey, if someone had told me that I needed to give up hours in my week to help a friend in need, I would have been skeptical about where to fit that time in. I was in the prime of my career, building my business with two kids at home, a three-year-old and a six-year-old. I thought I didn't have the time, but I still made it happen and was a better person for it—and it wasn't just me. There were many, many people who freely gave their time to Scott and Catie.

Scott's friends formed a board to start My Turn,

Scott's foundation to give back to others with ALS. There were many of us that regularly met to discuss how the board should look, the pros and cons of our messaging and how to be the most impactful. Soon, the board became *our turn* way to give back.

One person on the board, Chris, a successful restauranteur in Kalamazoo, suggested we change his annual golf tournament to benefit Scott, his family and the My Turn foundation. Through Chris's acts of giving to give, and along with those who showed up to the fundraiser, we were able to generate hundreds of thousands of dollars for Scott's family.

When my grandparents were still around, I happily gave the gift of time through lunches during my workday, which created some of our most treasured memories together. Looking back, I see how precious time must feel at that age. They must have been in their mid-80s, but they would drive to my office to come visit me. When they arrived, they would get out of the car very slowly and ask me to drive. I would carefully drive us all to a restaurant—perhaps to Big T's in Lawton for an olive burger or to Olive Garden for the breadsticks and lasagna. It didn't really matter where we were as long as we were together.

If you can give something to someone that means more to them than it does to you, do it. I say this to my kids almost daily. Giving to give is simple: be kind to others, give someone a compliment, make someone laugh, open a door, offer help, send a friendly text, volunteer your time and above all, be someone who has an optimistic attitude.

Every day, I think about something I can do to elevate just one person. It is surprisingly simple and will most certainly make your day just a little bit better. Justin Breen does this daily for someone very special in his life, namely his wife, Sarah.

In general, Justin's words are concise and straight to the point, with very little fluff in between. He spots things and blurts them out with little concern about what others will think. The thought of physical contact—like big hugs and expressions of empathy—makes him shiver. In fact, the thought likely never enters his mind. Still, even though big displays of affection make him uncomfortable, he is thoughtful and pushes himself to help others in ways that feel acceptable to him. In addition, he is a great listener—despite his frequent interruptions as he blurts out whatever enters his mind.

Back to Justin's wife Sarah. As she explained to me when we met in Necker, she once expressed to Justin that she needed words of affirmation to feel most loved. While this didn't come naturally to Justin (and still doesn't), he thought of a way that *would* come naturally to him to provide Sarah what she needed.

As a writer, Justin decided to start a journal. He would write an entry each day entirely devoted to Sarah. He pointed out the little things she did that he greatly appreciated. Justin continues to do this every day, which is no strain on him and is tremendously impactful to Sarah. In this instance, Justin is giving to give to his wonderful wife—not because he is asking for something in return but simply to make her feel loved.

As I have said before, giving does not have to involve money. However, if you can give monetarily, you can make even greater contributions that allow others to make a total transformation.

My giving tendencies began way back in my college years. I didn't have the money to give away but did it anyway, figuring I'd pay for it later. One such opportunity to give emerged in my relationship with my good friend, Dat.

A group of friends had decided to go to New York City for New Year's Eve. The plan was that we would all cobble our money together to share a room and wander the city for a few days. Dat was there when the idea was born, but unfortunately, I knew there was no possible way he would be able to afford the trip.

Around that same time, I got my very first credit card with a balance of $2,000. I had a job in college, per my parents' request, to cover the expenses that were not tuition related. My first purchase on that credit card were two airline tickets, one for me and one for Dat.

I knew that this experience would be life-changing for him. I had no idea how long it would take me to pay off that airline ticket, but my desire to give was so strong that it never crossed my mind to have Dat pay for it. He didn't ask for this gift, and as a result, his joy was a greater payback than anything else he could have given me.

My wife Lindsay and I had countless people that gave to us as it related to raising our kids, including my parents; Lindsay's mom, dad and stepmom; Sandy; Tom and Myrna; and our aunts and uncles. However, all these wonderful people led full lives. There were many other things they could have done with that time while still getting to develop relationships with their grandchildren, which made us appreciate their help all the more.

It is rewarding to give back to our loved ones, whether it be through time or gifts. On one occasion, my wife's stepmom Myrna was going to take a trip to Europe for a friend's wedding. She was thrilled for the trip, but she was concerned that she wouldn't get any sleep on the long flight. Lindsay and I found this to be the perfect time to give. We upgraded her to first class so she could enjoy the highest level of service, recline her seat and sleep as much as she liked.

The greatest way that one can give for the sake of giving is through mentorship and coaching. There have been countless times that others have done this for me, such as J Lo taking the time to share his stories for this book. For my part, I intend to continue to share my lessons as time marches on.

It is also important to instill this lesson into our children. This past year, Lindsay and I held our first "family summit" with our kids, Beckett and Avery. We set aside time to discuss our family beliefs and the importance of upholding our values, our purpose, our privilege and the responsibilities that come with them, as well as how we could more effectively help others.

For those of us with kids, it can sometimes be difficult to know if our messages are landing, but I was happy to see both of my children taking our lessons of giving to give seriously. Beckett had been tasked with selling candy bars for his middle school to raise money to send kids to camp. Half of what they raised would go to the camp funds, and the other half would go to the kids selling as an incentive for them to put in the work.

Shortly after selling his first box, Beckett was most excited about giving *all* the proceeds to the school after realizing that he could send many more kids to camp by donating his half. He also expanded his efforts to include other neighborhoods, which generated even more sales. He took his fundraising seriously, asking how many boxes it would take to send certain numbers of kids to camp.

For her part, Avery signed up for two programs at school, one of which was a pal's program to mentor younger kids, and another that involved working with disabled kids at her school. We were extremely proud of both of our children's commitments and felt that they were directly connected to what we had discussed during our family summit.

We all have something to share with someone and there is always someone who needs what we have to share—and we don't have to become successful business owners to do so. It can be as simple as helping someone solve a problem, driving them somewhere, cooking their favorite recipe, wrapping a present for them or helping them fix something.

Instead of thinking about all the money I could make and what kind of business I could start for personal gain, I try now to think about all the money I can give away. As discussed earlier, the thing that excites me most is giving braces to kids that can otherwise not afford them. Since we have started our foundation, I now dream of how to give on a much larger scale. Tom and I have created the medium to do this, but now we must weave that message into everything we do. It will be much more rewarding to see thousands of kids get braces than to see our net worth grow.

What drives me more than any financial gain is envisioning a day where I can meet thousands of kids with confident smiles. Now that we have worked hard to develop the networks and businesses to do these things at scale, it is exactly how we want to use our influence to make an impact.

As you think about this chapter, ask yourself: What are some things that you can do right away to give? I suggest starting small. See how it feels and then transform all your days to include giving. Remember: little movements in the right direction can make all the difference.

CHAPTER 7—BE ENDLESSLY GRATEFUL

Life is a gift.

There are reminders everywhere of how fortunate we are if we are willing to look for them. I exercise most days not due to an overwhelming desire to exercise, but because I *get* to.

Before and shortly after Scott fell ill, he was constantly pounding the pavement around the neighborhood and easily running five-minute miles. It was like he could see the sand running through the hourglass and was determined to maximize his physical abilities while he still had them.

When Scott could no longer run, he refused to sit down. He knew at some point that sitting would be his only option. He wanted to be able to stand on his own for as long as he could. As a friend, sometimes it was hard to keep up with him, as he was always on the go.

While Scott's timeline was short, he taught me a very important lesson: we never know when our natural gifts, skills and abilities will be stripped away from us. Because of that, we must maximize those gifts while we can and be very grateful for them while we are still able, regardless of what position we're in. We need not think about the things we can no longer do; instead, we should focus on the things we can still achieve.

After seeing Scott slowly decline, I no longer took my weekly exercise for granted. I was blessed to be able to use my arms and legs to propel myself into better shape. Not knowing how long I had to take advantage of my physical abilities motivated me to use them more often.

The same goes for mental acumen. People have an easier time getting ahead of eventual physical decline, but they don't as often think about mental decline; they believe that if they just continue to work hard, they can somehow completely avoid it. Still, the reality is that there are countless studies that suggest that mental decline starts for most people in their 20s and 30s.

We never know what changes might happen physically or mentally, so striving to take advantage of all the gifts we are given is crucial. We wouldn't want to look back and regret what we could have accomplished if we had only tried a little harder.

Our natural energy declines as we age. We may only have enough energy in the day to accomplish a fraction of what we could in decades past. My dad, my original mentor, often referenced this as he aged into his late 50s and early 60s. He had always taken great care of himself with his daily YMCA routine, which included running, playing paddleball and generally being active. Despite this daily routine, as time marched on, he would comment he simply didn't have the same energy at 60 that he once did.

My grandmother used to walk every day. She would start in her neighborhood and walk a few miles, rarely missing a day. I remember fondly her saying that she would continue to do her walks forever. If she could just pull herself up and out of the house, there would be little to stop her. Eventually, she did stop—not because she wanted to, but because at some point, her back, bones and muscles would no longer allow it.

I am grateful for the lessons that Scott, my dad and my grandmother taught me. If I want to be like them and maximize my abilities for as long as possible, I need to prioritize those things *now*—not next week, next month or next year. If you want to maximize the simple gifts you have been given, you need to put your plan into action. Think about it—what is holding you back?

At the time of this writing, my kids are 15 and 12. Part of the reason I exercise is because I want to be around for them for as long as I possibly can. I want to be able to keep up with them as they get older. I am very grateful that my parents showed me this lesson by example, through eating well and regularly exercising. My mom cooked us chicken and fish about 90 percent of the time. As much as my sister and I complained about it, my mom knew it would set good habits for us as we aged.

When my sister taught English in Japan after graduating college, we all went to visit her—she must have been 25 years old at the time, while I was 19 and our parents were around 52. One of our favorite memories from that trip was climbing Mount Fuji together. My parents were excited for the climb, although my mom caught altitude sickness on the way up. Had my parents not set an example for us on how to stay in shape and prioritize physical fitness, they never would have been able to keep up with us on that climb.

Summiting Mt. Fuji

There are many things I am grateful for. I am grateful for my friends; because we have always taken the time to nurture our relationships, there are many people who would show up for me if I needed them. I am grateful for my wife, Lindsay, who is constantly taking care of the kids and running the household, working, volunteering and making my life easier while still achieving her own personal happiness. When she is at her happiest, I am at mine.

I am grateful to have my amazing sister Sarah, who

was my living, breathing example of setting the bar high. She was my earliest source of motivation and taught me that if I wanted to succeed, I had to work hard for it. She was constantly working towards her goals—whether it was learning piano, earning her own money, striving to do well in school or surrounding herself with amazing people. In fact, she didn't even really *teach* me; she simply *showed* me firsthand.

I am grateful for the kindness of others. We live in a world where everyone expects so much, and few stop to think about the little things that people do for them. I am grateful for people who take the time to say hello, ask how my day is going or smile as they walk past me.

I am grateful for my assistant, Ann, who is constantly keeping me on track to live my purpose and achieve my goals. I am grateful for the ability to work and afford food for my family, as others in this world do not have food and clean water. I do not view cooking as a chore. Instead, I view it as a reward that many do not have. I like to try new recipes because I am able to, not because I have to.

I am grateful to my doctor for suggesting new ways that my family and I can stay on top of our health. These are things that I would not be able to discover on my own.

I am grateful to my dentist for cleaning my teeth and my hair stylist for cutting my hair, which keeps me presentable and feeling good. I am grateful when people deliver my mail and packages on time—and when they do not, I am grateful that it wasn't because they were in an accident.

I am grateful for the hardest times in my life. Each challenge has given me knowledge and perspective that I would not have had otherwise. If you have never experienced a fall, you have never experienced pulling yourself back up. One of life's greatest joys is the ascent.

If I am going through a hard time, regardless of how big or small, I am grateful. Whenever I'm down, I envision how good my comeback will eventually feel. Nothing lasts forever, and if you can just imagine yourself succeeding after a setback, you will start to embrace the journey and appreciate all of life's ebbs and flows.

Time moves fast. When you think about your life, 10 years ago likely does not seem like that long ago. You were *just* there—yet an entire decade has passed. Ten years, 20 years, even 30 years goes by very, very fast—and that is assuming we will even get 30 more years to accomplish the things we want to achieve. There is no time to procrastinate, and there is certainly no time to complain.

Appreciate everything in your world. As Dan Sullivan and Dr. Benjamin Hardy said in *The Gap and the Gain*, "Proactive gratitude is about appreciating everything in the world around you. It's not initiated by something special the world first does for you, but rather by something special that you first do for the world."[1] Their book has been hugely influential on how I view gratitude in my life.

In the 1946 Frank Capra film *It's a Wonderful Life*, an angel named Clarence appears to a man named George Bailey who is about to jump off a bridge and end his life.

---

1. Sullivan, Dan. 2021. *Gap and the Gain*. S.L.: Hay House Business.

Clarence takes George through a spiritual tour of the world as it would have been if George was never born.

Clarence allows George to see all the ripples and repercussions that would have occurred if he hadn't been born. George is allowed to see a world devoid of all the good things he'd done. By imagining the *absence* of everything good in his life, George realizes just how rare and precious the good things are. His outlook on life *instantly* changes.

Psychologists have tested whether the absence of the good things in your life could make you appreciate them more—a concept called *mental subtraction*. The results are clear: Mental subtraction is one of the most effective and science-based techniques for boosting our gratitude and happiness.

Likewise, imagining the absence of an important person in your life can be more powerful than simply appreciating the fact that they are there. One study found that mentally subtracting a material possession you've previously enjoyed increases your happiness with that item more than simply thinking back on when you purchased it.

Research also shows that when it comes to romantic relationships, those who never imagined meeting their romantic partner reported far higher levels of relationship satisfaction after doing the mental subtraction exercise.[2]

---

2. Sullivan, Dan. 2021. *Gap and the Gain*. S.L.: Hay House Business.

To try this out, ask yourself some of these questions:

- *What if right now, you lost your good health?*
- *Or if you could no longer walk?*
- *Or if you went blind?*
- *Think about a very important person in your life. What if right now, that person died?*
- *What if you'd never met that person in the first place?*
- *How different would your life be?*

It's all too easy to take our lives for granted, which is why mental subtraction is so crucial. By imagining that the important people and things in your life don't exist, you can genuinely start to appreciate what you have. By imagining that your greatest achievements or progress never occurred, you can see how far you have come.

With all this in mind, what things are you grateful for? Who are the people in your life that have made a difference for you? What abilities do you have that others would be thrilled to have? Are you taking any of them for granted? What will you do, right now, to change these things? How will you use your abilities or reach out to people you may otherwise be taking for granted?

STOP HITTING SNOOZE

CONCLUSION

So, where do you go from here? Start big or start small, but *start somewhere*. As my grandfather always told us:

"Do something, even if it's wrong!"

Make a commitment to yourself and have the discipline to back it up. Realize that while it may be impossible to attain balance all at once, and perhaps impossible to completely master at all, even getting close will feel great.

Understand that at times, you will fail, and that is perfectly okay. Remember to give yourself grace, as change is hard, and it does not follow a linear path.

Remember that sometimes, you will be in the fluctuation zone, which is normal when making a change. Work hard not to cross the line of despair, but understand that if you do, you can absolutely get back to the ideal zone.

In other words:

Face the fear of failure and the fear of regret. Build a future that is bigger than your past.

As I learned through my friends Scott and Adam, life is precious and exceptionally short. If we are to live our lives to the fullest, we need to take action right away to *discover our purpose.*

The great news is it is never too late to start. There are so many people I know who are in their 40s, 50s and 60s who constantly talk about the "good old days," as if they are times of great happiness that can never be achieved again. What if, for a moment, you thought that you were *in* the good old days *right now?*

In other words: it's the day you are living right now that matters most. Not yesterday, not tomorrow, but right now. Striving to lead a life of purpose and to consistently remain balanced will help you to be present with this fact.

Regardless of where you are in life, I fundamentally believe that your best days are always ahead of you. So much time is wasted on simply going through the motions of life, but the most precious moments are with the people we love.

At some point in the future, we will not have the same energy or mental capacity to do the things we are able to do today. What a shame it would be to waste the time we have now to continue to learn and grow.

I often think about the questions I will ask myself later in life—did I strive to accomplish everything I could? Did I take advantage of the gifts that I was given, and did I maximize those gifts? Did I pull myself up when things got off track to attempt to become a better person? Did I help as many people as I could along the way? Do I feel good about the legacy I'm leaving behind? How will I be remembered?

Being remembered as somebody that was successful is great, but there will always be someone more successful than you. The true mark of being great is helping others become the best versions of themselves: to learn valuable lessons, teach others what you have learned and give in any way that you can. If you can accomplish these things, you will truly be a success. As I said before, start big or start small, but *start somewhere:*

> *Discover your purpose...*
> *Be relentlessly determined to strive for balance...*
> *Do not be afraid to leave your old identity behind—*
> *face your fears and become better for it...*
> *Nurture your friendships and foster new ones...*
> *Know that you always control the outcome...*
> *Give to give, not to get...*
> *Remain endlessly grateful...*

After all:

Life is short, and there is no time to waste.

ACKNOWLEDGMENTS

This book wouldn't have been possible without the support and guidance of many over the years.

First and foremost, thank you to my wife, Lindsay and my two amazing kids, Avery and Beckett. Thank you to my unbelievable parents and original mentors, Bob and Judy, and my inspiring sister, Sarah, for their unwavering support. Thank you to my brother-in-law, Matt, for always encouraging me to take risks and push myself. A big tip of the hat to Justin Breen, who pushed me to write this when I didn't think I had the time or thought of doing so!

I also thank my friend Mike M., who inspired me to think about many of the topics in this book and for being incredibly open to me sharing this story.

Thank you to my extended family, who always show me what real love looks and feels like.

Thank you to my friends, both those who have been here since the start and those I have become close with in more recent years—your support, advice and guidance over the course of my life is irreplaceable.

Thank you to Shane, Rod and J Lo, who graciously gave up their time so I could share their stories for my book.

Thank you, Tom, for continually pushing me to places I otherwise would not have gone.

Thank you, Tim, for giving me opportunities I otherwise would not have had.

Thank you to those who have trusted me to get to know them, guide them and to bless me with their shared perspective along the way.

And finally, a big thank you to my publisher, Anna David, and her amazing team at Legacy Launch Pad Publishing, who guided me and helped me make this book a reality.

ABOUT THE AUTHOR

Brant Shrimplin is a founder, entrepreneur and published author. His career in wealth management started in 1999 in New York City on the NYSE floor. In 2009, Brant founded 626 Financial, a Registered Investment Advisor based out of Kalamazoo, MI. His entrepreneurial spirit evolved to include privately held investments, with a particular focus on real estate and venture fund investing for high-net-worth families across the US. Brant lives with his wife Lindsay and their two children in Kalamazoo, Michigan. *Stop Hitting Snooze* is his first book.

1,000 sets of braces for 1,000 kids in 1,000 days. There are moments in time that are life-changing. For many kids, this comes in the form of braces, a confidence-inspiring moment during life's pivotal years. Unfortunately, the ability to receive this gift is out of reach for many. Please join us in our mission to change that one smile at a time.

Legacy Launch Pad is a boutique publishing company that works with entrepreneurs from all over the world. For more information about Legacy Launch Pad Publishing, go to: www.legacylaunchpadpub.com

Printed in the USA
CPSIA information can be obtained
at www.ICGtesting.com
LVHW091508021124
795332LV00008B/188/J

9 781964 377285